I0427616

TABLE OF CONTENTS

ILLUSTRATION

TABLE

LIST OF ACRONYMS

AF   Agreed Framework

CPI   Counterproliferation Initiative

DPRK   Democratic People's Republic of Korea, also referred to as North Korea

EMIS   Electron-magnetic Isotope Separation

FAS   Feasibility, Acceptability, and Suitability

GMR   Graphite-moderated Reactor

HFO   Heavy Fuel Oil, also referred to as residual fuel oil.

KEDO   Korean Peninsula Energy Development Organization

KEPCO   Korean Electric Power Company

KWP   Korean Workers' Party

IAEA   International Atomic Energy Agency

NBC   Nuclear, Biological and Chemical

PCP   Preemptive Counterproliferation

PDD   Presidential Decision Directive

PNI   Presidential Nuclear Initiative

PWR   Pressurized-Water Reactor

ROK   Republic of Korea or South Korea

TD   Transmission and Distribution

UN   United Nations

UNIR   United Institute for Nuclear Research

WMD   Weapon of Mass Destruction

CHAPTER 1

INTRODUCTION

On 6 August 1945, a new chapter was written in the annals of warfare--atomic war--when

Hiroshima, Japan, became the first city to be attacked with an atomic weapon. This attack by the

United States (US) was followed three days later by a second atomic attack on Nagasaki. These

dual attacks quickly precipitated the Japanese surrender on 2 September 1945, which marked the

end of the Second World War. After the war other nations worked to develop atomic (nuclear)

arms. In 1949 the Soviet Union became the world's second nuclear power and by 1964, Great

Britain, France, and China had all tested and produced nuclear weapons.

The rising specter of nuclear weapons proliferation inspired the United Nations (UN) to

propose an international treaty designed to halt such proliferation. The result was the

Nonproliferation Treaty (NPT) of 1970. This treaty, currently signed by 187 nations, while

holding that it is illegal for any but the original five nuclear states to either manufacture or posses

nuclear weapons, also obligates these same five nations to work towards the eventual goal of

totally eliminating their nuclear weapons stockpile. The UN organ tasked with the oversight of

this treaty is the International Atomic Energy Agency (IAEA), which is vested with the

responsibility to verify (by way of inspections) that treaty signatories (excluding the original five

nuclear states) are not developing nuclear weapons programs.

The US embraces the nonproliferation of nuclear weapons as a vital national interest,

and, consequently, it aggressively applies its instruments of national power to prevent and deter

the proliferation of nuclear weapons. In this endeavor the US has experienced varying degrees of

success. Although the US was unable to prevent Israel, India, and Pakistan from acquiring

nuclear arms, because of their friendly or nonaggressive relations towards the US their emergence

as nuclear powers has been somewhat tolerated. However, this position of tolerance has not been

extended to nations that are hostile towards the US, such as Iraq, Iran, and North Korea (the official name is the Democratic People's Republic of Korea (DPRK)). On the contrary, the US, working both unilaterally and multilaterally, has actively attempted to prevent these and other "rogue nations" from acquiring nuclear weapons.

In 1992, during an IAEA full-scope safeguards inspection at North Korea's Yongbyon Nuclear Research Center, an IAEA team discovered that North Korea had secretly diverted reprocessed weapons-grade plutonium from its five-megawatt nuclear reactor (Mazarr 1995,94). This discovery prompted North Korea to expel all of the IAEA inspectors, cancel all safeguards inspections, and submit a ninety-day letter of resignation signifying its intent to withdraw from the NPT. Consequently, the US was plunged into a crisis, as it sought to stop an assumed North Korean attempt to produce nuclear weapons.

Although initially unclear exactly how to resolve the crisis because of the potential threat of a nuclear-armed North Korean regime, the US understood the need for action. At risk was the military and economic security of Japan and South Korea. There was the potential for a Northeast Asia nuclear arms race. An equal threat was a North Korean regime that could credibly challenge US regional security measures in several areas. A threat of nuclear attack upon Japan might restrict the US from using military bases in Japan to counter a North Korean invasion of South Korea. Furthermore, an economically destitute North Korea, which relied on robust weapons sales to other rogue nations, might find the sale of nuclear weapons, nuclear weapons material, or nuclear weapons technology to other enemies of the US to be financially rewarding.

What followed over the next two years was a Clinton administration effort to convince Pyongyang to abandon its nuclear weapons program. In October 1994, the US and North Korea signed their first and only bilateral accord, the Agreed Framework. Under the terms of this agreement, North Korea, in exchange for a package deal that included the transfer of two light-water nuclear reactors from the US, agreed to freeze and ultimately dismantle its nuclear weapons development capabilities.

This event was significant because of international concern over antiquated GMR nuclear reactors used by North Korea and its capability to separate weapons-grade plutonium. At the Yongbyon Nuclear Research Center was a plutonium reprocessing facility, two operational graphite-moderated reactors, one five-megawatt electric reactor and one eight-megawatt research reactor, and under construction was one fifty-megawatt graphite-moderated reactor. At Taechon a 200-megawatt graphite-moderated reactor was under construction.

With the signing of the Agreed Framework, both sides agreed to cooperate to replace North Korea's two existing nuclear reactors and the two nuclear reactors under construction with two light-water reactor (LWR) power plants. Additionally, agreements were made to provide 500,000 metric tons of heavy fuel per annum until the first LWR became operational, move toward full normalization of political and economic relations, and work together for peace and security on a nuclear-free Korean Peninsula.

The Agreed Framework is in its eighth year. The LWR project, originally contracted for completion in 2003, is still many years from completion, heavy fuel oil (HFO) shipments are habitually delivered late, continued shipments are at risk, and economic and political normalization has not been addressed. Consequently, North Korea's reactor-based nuclear weapons program, though frozen, has not been dismantled. Additionally, because North Korea continues to prohibit full-scope safeguards inspections, the IAEA is unable to confirm the status of North Korea's nuclear weapons program and how much fissile material North Korea possesses. Therefore, these and other issues continue to place at risk the successful completion of the Agreed Framework--the US policy instrument for achieving the permanent or long-term denuclearization of North Korea. Accordingly, the question of how the US should proceed in this endeavor, to effectively achieve this national interest, is one of great national significance.

Research Objective

Primary Research Question

The principal focus of this study is, first, to outline the problems challenging the continued effectiveness of the 1994 Agreed Framework and, second, to evaluate alternative policy options to eliminate North Korea's nuclear weapons program.

Subordinate Research Questions

As a supporting effort, the following questions assist in understanding the thesis topic:

1. What is the historical context in which the Agreed Framework was written?

2. What are the alternative policy options to the Agreed Framework?

3. Why was the Agreed Framework written?

4. What are the contractual clauses of the Agreed Framework?

5. What progress has or has not developed on the Agreed Framework?

6. What are the ancillary effects of the Agreed Framework?

Limitation

The bulk of existing literature published in English provides only the views of the American, South Korean, and Russian experts. There is only a small collection of material that presents the Japanese, Chinese, and North Korean perspectives, including Internet and third party reports.

Delimitation

Though a detailed presentation of how each of the six principal players (US, South Korea, North Korea, Japan, China, and Russia) view this issue would be ideal, it is beyond the scope of this paper. Accordingly, it is the view from the US that will be the focus of the paper. This thesis will also not cover the scientific aspects of nuclear power plant construction or the refining process of weapons-grade plutonium. This thesis is limited to documents that were written or translated in English and made available by 31 January 2002.

Sources

Seven years have passed since the signing of the Agreed Framework. Though the agreement and the events leading up to it could be categorized as recent history, this issue is probably more accurately categorized as a current event. Since 1995, only four books that explicitly focus on the story of the North Korean atomic bomb have been published. These books, in chronological order, are: (1) Michael J. Mazarr, 1995, *North Korea and the Bomb*; (2) Young Whan Kihl and Peter Hayes, 1997, *Peace and Security in Northeast Asia: The Nuclear Issue and the Korean Peninsula;* (3) Leon V. Sigal, 1998, *Disarming Strangers: Nuclear Diplomacy with North Korea;* and (4) James C. Moltz and Alexander Y. Mansourov, 2000, *The North Korean Nuclear Program: Security, Strategy, and New Perspectives from Russia.*

In addition to these four focused works, four others provide good insight into this topic, including: (1) Mitchell Reiss, 1995, *Bridled Ambition*; (2) Don Oberdorfer, 1997, *The Two Koreas: A Contemporary History*; (3) Thomas H. Henriksen and Mo Jongryn, 1997, *North Korea after Kim Il Sung: Continuity or Change?* and (4) Suh Dae Sook and Lee Chae Jin, 1998, *North Korea after Kim Il Sung.*

These eight books are complemented by three other categories of research material: US government and international organization reports, periodicals and Internet papers, and military service school theses and monographs. An excellent paper on possible solutions to the problem entitled "The Korean Peninsula Energy Development Organization: Achievement and Challenges" was written in 1999 by Joel S. Wit, the Agreed Framework Coordinator in the US Department of State, Bureau of East Asia and Pacific Affairs. Because of the currency of this issue, the Internet and periodicals serve as an invaluable resource of information. The enclosed reference list includes all web pages and publications that were found to be particularly beneficial in researching this topic.

Significance of the Study

After Pyongyang notified the world on 12 March 1993 of its intent to withdraw from the NPT, the US began a major effort to keep North Korea from further work on developing nuclear weapons. The scope of considered policy options ranged from diplomatic dialogue to the imposition of economic sanctions and the graduated escalation of armed military conflict. The possible use of military force during this crisis was not a radical option, but rather a serious point of discussion.

The following year, on 19 March 1994, during a North-South working level meeting at Panmunjom, North Korean negotiator, Pak Yong Su stormed out of the Military Armistice Commission (MAC) building threatening "Seoul is not far from here. If a war breaks out, it will be a sea of fire" (Oberdorfer 1997, 304). As the world reeled from this bellicose remark, Seoul reacted by heightening defensive measures, and the US reacted by deploying a Patriot missile battery to the Korean Peninsula. Pak Yong Su's threat ominously echoed a US Central Intelligence Agency report given to President Clinton five months earlier. In essence, the report declared that North Korea had already produced one or two nuclear bombs. Consequently, as tensions mounted and fear escalated, the US, in a move to placate regional tensions, pressed Pyongyang for continued discussions. What eventually ensued, after a series of many high-level talks, was the Agreed Framework.

The Agreed Framework has been lambasted by many as compromising and expensive, and so it might be. However, the use of direct pressure (economic sanctions, preemptive strikes) might, as many have suggested, inadvertently intensify the situation and cause the outbreak of a second Korean War that would be no less tasking to both the United States' mettle and fiscal resources than the hostilities of 1950-1953. General Luck, a former commander of the United States Forces Korea (USFK), estimated that war on the peninsula would exact as many as one million casualties, including the loss of 80,000 to 100,000 Americans, and at a cost of $100 billion to the US. Additionally, he estimated that the destruction of property and the interruption of business activities would cost more than $1 trillion to countries within the region (Oberdorfer 1997, 324).

The importance of this issue is clear. The value of this study, in its application among politicians, strategic planners, and regional experts, is primarily twofold. First, this thesis assesses the state of the Agreed Framework, and second, it evaluates alternative policy options for halting the proliferation of nuclear weapons in North Korea.

Summary

The eleventh of September 2001 marked the beginning of a new era. America felt the power of a nonstate (terrorist group), and indeed, that ripple has spread to democratic nations everywhere. For the first time since the War of 1812, the American homeland was attacked. This attack may encourage other terrorist groups or rogue nations to exploit the weaknesses. For many Americans, the demise of the Soviet Union created a sense of security, a feeling that the homeland was beyond an enemy's reach. Now, since the terrorist attacks of 11 September, the exposed vulnerability makes it easier to conceive of an attack upon America by a rogue state, like North Korea. Today, more than ever, it is resoundingly clear that, among security issues where failure could have unrecoverable ramifications, proliferation of nuclear weapons stands foremost. As such, it is paramount that a nuclear threat by North Korea be eliminated.

As stated, this thesis will examine the Agreed Framework, identify successes and failures in its implementation, and determine if it is achieving its intended purpose--the permanent or long-term denuclearization of North Korea. Finally, three alternative policy options are presented and analyzed for halting the proliferation of nuclear weapons in North Korea.

Synopsis of Chapters 2 through 5

Chapter 2. Although the threat created by the North Korean nuclear program is a relatively recent issue, many authoritative works on it have been published. This chapter summarizes the key events leading up to the signing of the Agreed Framework. It also examines the Agreed Framework and the steps taken to turn the agreement into reality.

Chapter 3. Chapter 3 discusses four possible approaches to the permanent or long-term denuclearization of North Korea. These policy options are: (1) continuing with the Agreed Framework; (2) amending the Agreed Framework; (3) adopting a more comprehensive framework; and (4) undertaking a coercive denuclearization option. This chapter describes how these options will be evaluated using the FAS (feasibility, acceptability, and suitability) test.

Chapter 4. Chapter 4 analyzes each denuclearization policy option in terms of: (1) the feasibility of it being adequately implemented; (2) its acceptability to the parties involved; and (3) its suitability for achieving the denuclearization of North Korea, without the advent of war, and contributing to the *National Security Strategy* objectives of the US in Northeast Asia. These objectives are: (1) promoting the nuclear nonproliferation regime; (2) enhancing the security of allies; and (3) maintaining the US influence in Northeast Asia (Clinton 2000, 4-9).

Chapter 5. Chapter 5 contains conclusions and recommendations for achieving the permanent or long-term denuclearization of North Korea.

CHAPTER 2

HISTORICAL BACKGROUND OF NORTH KOREA'S NUCLEAR PROGRAM AND THE AGREED FRAMEWORK

The Quest to Build a Nuclear Bomb: Historical Context

A People Divided

At the end of the Second World War the US and the former Soviet Union divided the Korean Peninsula at the 38th Parallel for the purpose of accepting the surrender of Japanese military units. This event had the unintended consequence of dividing a homogenous people and sending them down diverging paths. In short, the US occupation of the southern portion of the Korean Peninsula led to the establishment of South Korea, a democratic nation with a free-enterprise economy, while the former Soviet Union's occupation of the northern part led to the creation of North Korea, a communist nation. Within two years of the creation of these antithetical countries, North Korea conducted a surprise attack upon South Korea, plunging the two countries and several allied nations into a bloody three-year war. This war exacted over four million casualties (Oberdorfer 1997, 10) and forged a mutual perpetual hatred and mistrust that festers still today.

In December 1950, when the UN forces reeled from the Chinese offensive and later when the Korean War had stagnated along the 38th parallel, President Truman contemplated using nuclear weapons in Korea. In early 1953, President Eisenhower went so far as to actually threaten the use of nuclear weapons (George and Smoke 1974, 235-238). A well-documented indirect threat to China occurred during an exchange between Secretary of State John Dulles and India's leader Jawaharal Nehru. In May 1953, Dulles, speaking about the Panmunjom Talks, stated that the US would use "stronger rather than lesser" military means if conflict resolution could not be agreed upon (Dingman 1988, 79-86). Two months later, on 27 July 1953, the US, China, and North Korea signed an armistice agreement. Whether or not there was a direct link between Dulles's words and the Chinese agreement to an armistice, both President Eisenhower and

9

Secretary of State Dulles attributed the ending of the Korean War to a threat to use atomic weapons (Mazarr 1995, 16). Hence, the lesson that a country possessing nuclear power had the ability to force its will upon those that did not was not lost on either North Korea or China.

United States Displays of Force against North Korea

In the decades since the Korean War, American presidents have threatened North Korea with armed retaliation several times, but have never actually employed arms. On 23 January 1968, the USS *Pueblo*, on an intelligence collection mission off the coast of North Korea, was attacked and subsequently captured. As a show of force, the US deployed to the region three battle groups and hundreds of fighter planes, including strategic bombers. However, in the end, President Lyndon B. Johnson ordered no military action, and a crew of eighty-two, one of whom died of wounds, remained in captivity for eleven months.

During President Nixon's administration, 15 April 1969, an American EC-121 spy plane, flying missions near North Korea, was shot down with its crew of thirty men over the East Sea. Four months later the North Koreans shot down an OH-53. That event ended in the US issuing a letter of apology to the North Korean government in exchange for the three wounded airmen. In August 1976, during the presidency of Gerald Ford, the North Koreans savagely used axes to kill two US Army officers and to wound eight soldiers during an unprovoked incident in the Joint Security Area of the demilitarized zone (DMZ). In a show of force, the US flew B52 bombers over the DMZ.

President Jimmy Carter, well remembered for his attempts to remove the American military presence from Korea, also threatened to use military forces against North Korea. Following the assassination of South Korean President Pak Jung Hee by South Korea's Central Intelligence Director Kim Jae Kyu on 26 October 1979, the US deployed a carrier battle group to the waters of South Korea and conducted practice bombing runs, dropping eleven practice nuclear rounds into the ocean (Hahn 2000, 6). Lastly, in 1994, because of North Korea's nuclear weapons program, President Clinton seriously contemplated a preemptive strike against North Korea.

From the North Korean view, there were also two ongoing threats: forward-deployed nuclear weapons, which were in South Korea from 1956 until 1991, and the annual US-ROK bilateral military exercise--Team Spirit, conducted from 1976 until 1991. None of this, however, has been sufficient to end provocative acts by North Korea. Through the last fifty years there has been unflinching defiance from, first, Kim Il Sung and then his son and successor, Kim Jong Il.

The Search for Nuclear Knowledge

On 6 May 1952, the Soviet Union and North Korea signed an education agreement authorizing North Korean students the opportunity to matriculate at Soviet institutions of higher learning (undergraduate and graduate level). In 1956, just four years later, in the city of Dubna (near Moscow), the Soviet Union established the United Institute for Nuclear Research (UINR) to serve as its international and research center for socialist countries (Zhebin 2000, 28-29). It was at this institution that North Korea, by educating its cadre, took its first step towards nuclear weapons development. Since the founding of UINR, more than 250 North Koreans have graduated from the institution.

Though many North Korean scientists have been trained at various international scientific institutions, such as those in the former Soviet Union, Japan, China, and both the former German Democratic Republic and the Federal Republic of Germany, many have also studied at domestic educational facilities. North Korea's principal nuclear research complex, the Pyongsong Atomic Energy Research Center, is located in Pyongsong, fifty kilometers north of Pyongyang. This complex houses seventeen research institutes and one experimental test facility. Among the institutes, the Pyongsong College of Science, Nuclear Physics Department is the principal institution and employs a staff of five to six thousand. Among North Korea's other scientific institutes, four are major contributors to nuclear development. They include the Institutes of

Physics, the Institute of Mathematics, the Institute of Electronic Control Machines, and the Institute of Electronics. The State Committee on Science and Technology, chaired by Choi Hee Cheng, supervises these and all other nuclear research institutions. The Institute of Physics was founded in 1952 and as of 2000 had a staff of 250 (Denisov 2000, 23). The director, Dr. Cho Chen Nam, is a specialist in laser physics. Among the school's principal research efforts are: (1) lasers and optics, (2) the physics of solids, (3) changes in the properties of materials under extreme conditions--high pressures, low temperatures, and vacuums, and (4) acoustics and surface waves. Additionally, Dr. Nam Hong Woo, a faculty member, conducted research on a solution to the Bolzmann Equation for the description of Uranium-235 and Uranium-238 fission processes (Denisov 2000, 24). The Institute of Mathematics, established in the 1960s, has several laboratories that focus on programming, mathematical physics, differential equations, quantitative modeling, computational and fundamental mathematics, and the mechanics of liquids and gases. The Institute of Electronic Control Machines, which was established in 1984, contributes to the development of production systems. The Institute of Electronics develops large integrated computer circuits and as of 2000 employed a staff of 402 specialists (Denisov 2000, 25).

Construction of Nuclear Facilities

In 1959 the Soviets and North Koreans signed the "Series 9559" contract, an intergovernmental atomic energy cooperation agreement. The agreement had three basic elements: (1) geological studies of North Korea, (2) construction of a nuclear research center, and (3) the training of Korean specialists (Kaurov 2000, 15).

In accordance with the aforementioned agreement, Soviet scientists conducted a site survey in order to identify an area that was suitable to house a nuclear reactor. The area selected was Yongbyon, because of its resistance to earthquakes (greater than 8.0 on the Richter scale), but the team failed to take into consideration flooding, an issue that continues to plague the site. Today, the Yongbyon Scientific Research Center is a complex of over one hundred buildings. In the first phase of construction, Soviet specialists built an IRT-2000 nuclear research reactor, a radiochemical laboratory, a K-60,000 cobalt installation, and a B-25 betatron. In 1965, construction began on the IRT-2000, a two-megawatt reactor. By 1967, the aforementioned Soviet-built nuclear research reactor was operational. Later it was upgraded by Korean scientists, first to a capacity of five megawatts, and then to its current capacity of eight megawatts (Zhebin 2000, 31). In 1974 the reactor came under the supervisory auspices of the IAEA as North Korea officially signed the IAEA's Information Circular Form-66, Facility-Based Safeguards Agreement (Mazarr 1995, 25).

In 1970, at the Fifth Congress of the Korean Workers' Party (KWP) and again at the Sixth Congress in 1980, delegates stressed the desirability and necessity of developing a nuclear power program to sharply increase the generation of electrical power. North Korea is rich in natural uranium (twenty-six million tons of reserves) and graphite deposits, but lacks significant oil deposits or consistent hydroelectric and thermal-electric capabilities. Consequently, the national leadership decided to develop a nuclear energy program based on gas-graphite reactors, which can be powered with unenriched uranium and moderated with graphite (Denisov 2000, 22).

In 1980, North Korea began construction on Yongbyon Reactor-2, a five-megawatt nuclear reactor. Four years into this project, North Korea assumed a more ambitious role by constructing Yongbyon Reactor-3, a fifty-megawatt reactor, followed shortly thereafter by a 200-megawatt reactor at Taechon, neither of which was ever completed.

In 1985, the Soviet and North Korean governments signed a nuclear reactor construction contract titled the Agreement on Economic and Technical Cooperation in the Construction of a Nuclear Power Plant in North Korea. Under the terms of the agreement, North Korea agreed to pay for Soviet assistance in constructing four VVER-440 type reactors (Soviet version of the PWR). By early 1992, the Soviet construction team had finished both the site survey at Sinpo and the technical design of the project. However, during the site preparation stage, North Korea fell

13

behind on its payments, resulting in the suspension of the project. Finally, with no apparent method of repaying the estimated $1.7 to $4.7 million debt, North Korea declared the contract void, stating that the Russian Confederation was a different country after the collapse of the Soviet Union (Kaurov 2000, 19).

Today, there are reportedly as many as twenty-two nuclear facilities of various sorts in eighteen locations in North Korea. These include uranium mines, refinery plants, nuclear fuel plants, nuclear reactors, reprocessing facilities, and research facilities. Figure 1 lists all known related nuclear sites.

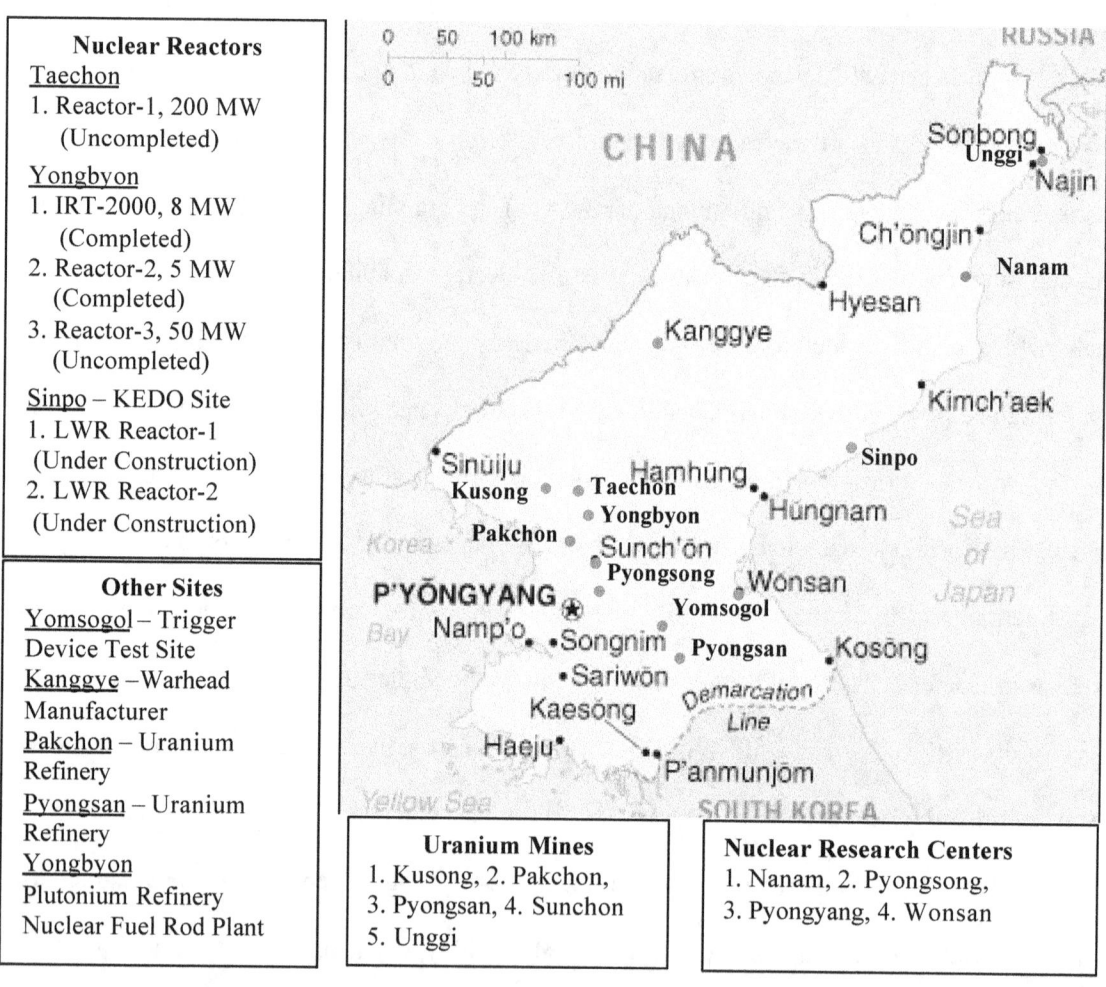

Nuclear Reactors
Taechon
1. Reactor-1, 200 MW
   (Uncompleted)
Yongbyon
1. IRT-2000, 8 MW
   (Completed)
2. Reactor-2, 5 MW
   (Completed)
3. Reactor-3, 50 MW
   (Uncompleted)
Sinpo – KEDO Site
1. LWR Reactor-1
(Under Construction)
2. LWR Reactor-2
(Under Construction)

Other Sites
Yomsogol – Trigger
Device Test Site
Kanggye –Warhead
Manufacturer
Pakchon – Uranium
Refinery
Pyongsan – Uranium
Refinery
Yongbyon
Plutonium Refinery
Nuclear Fuel Rod Plant

Uranium Mines
1. Kusong, 2. Pakchon,
3. Pyongsan, 4. Sunchon
5. Unggi

Nuclear Research Centers
1. Nanam, 2. Pyongsong,
3. Pyongyang, 4. Wonsan

Figure 1. Map of North Korean Related Nuclear Sites. Sources: Central Intelligence Agency *World Factbook* WebPages and Federation of American Scientists WebPages

From Nuclear Power to Nuclear Weapons

In the 1970s, according to a Soviet intelligence report, Kim Il Sung ordered North Korea's Academy of Sciences to build nuclear weapons (Hahn 2000, 14). Knowing when North Korea began its nuclear weapons program provides an estimate as to the earliest date at which they might have built a nuclear warhead. Though the US was able to build an atomic bomb in only four years, on average it has taken other nations six to seven years to build a bomb after having acquired fissionable material. In 1993, Director Central Intelligence R. James Woolsey claimed that North Korea possessed enough plutonium to manufacture one or two bombs (Zhebin 2000, 35). However, three years earlier, in 1990, the Soviet *Komityet Gosudarstvyennoj Byezopasnosti* (KGB), in a secret document, reported to the Central Committee of the Communist Party that the North Koreans had already created its first nuclear explosive device. Hahn Ho Suk, the Director of the New York based Center for (South) Korean Affairs, provides compelling evidence to support his thesis that North Korea built its first nuclear bomb in 1986.

Hahn's point of argument centers on three elements: North Korean nuclear scientists, engineering, and time lines. Hahn Ho Suk credits three prominent scientists, Doctors Lee Sung Ki, Do Sang Rok, and Han In Suk, with building the bomb. Dr. Lee (1905-1996), a chemist, was the first director of North Korea's Atomic Energy Agency, and he led the nation's nuclear weapons program. Dr. Do (1903-1990), an internationally published quantum field theorist, built a particle accelerator and conducted North Korea's first experiment on nuclear reactions. Dr. Han (born circa 1905) studied physics in Japan and Germany before World War II. After the Korean War, he studied physics at Moscow University. He returned to Pyongyang in 1960 and published numerous research papers on nuclear physics. In addition to these renowned scientists, several hundred other scientists studied in the Soviet Union (Hahn 2000, 12).

North Korea's engineering technology is fairly advanced. In 1961, it built its first electric-train and was building MiG-15 airplane parts. In 1970, it was building T-59 tanks, RPG-7 antitank rockets, 180-millimeter self-propelled field guns, 152-millimeter howitzers, and 1,500-ton frigates. By 1975, it had built its first submarine and had begun developing Frog missiles and K61 amphibious armored vehicles. In 1980 it began construction on Yongbyon Reactor-2, a five-megawatt reactor and by 1987 placed it into operation. In 1984, it began construction on Yongbyon Reactor-3, a fifty-megawatt reactor (Hahn 2000, 13-14).

In considering the time line, both Pakistan and North Korea embarked on a nuclear weapons program at about the same time. By 1992, Pakistan, which is inferior to North Korea in military technology, announced that it had created a nuclear explosive device. In 1974, South Korea, a technological competitor with the North, began its nuclear weapons program. Had the US not insisted on the halting of that program, South Korea would have built its first nuclear bomb in the 1980s. Following this line of logic, Hahn Ho Suk presents a thought-provoking view as to both the possibility and the time line of North Korea's possession of nuclear weapons.

Nuclear Bomb Construction 101

The ability to employ a nuclear warhead requires three distinct requirements: the first is the possession of fissionable material, the second is the ability to split or fission atoms, and the third is the ability to delivery a payload (payload delivery capabilities are discussed in chapter 4).

Two manufactured substances, uranium-235 (U-235) and plutonium-239 (PU-239), are practical for producing fissionable material. Of the two, uranium-235 is more difficult to produce. On average, seven-tenths of 1 percent of natural uranium ore is U-235. Separating U-235 from the ore is made difficult by the presence of a similar material--uranium-238. Because of the presence of these like elements, a specialized separation process is required. There are three highly technical methods of U-235 separation--centrifuge, laser, and nozzle separation. These processes are expensive, time consuming, and, as stated, require a sophisticated scientific and industrial capability. Consequently, these processes are considered prohibitively difficult among developing nations.

In addition to the highly technical methods of uranium separation, there are two simpler methods--gaseous diffusion and electron-magnetic isotope separation (EMIS). Gaseous diffusion, the process employed during the Manhattan Project, is a procedure that forces gaseous uranium, uranium hexafluoride ($UF6$), through a porous barrier. Because of the rate of seepage or diffusion, U-235 seeps through quicker than U-238. This process of separation is very tedious. During the Manhattan Project, 4,000 separate diffusions were required to produce weapons-grade material. The second method is EMIS. This process, also used during the Manhattan Project, requires the use of a machine called a calutron. Employing huge magnets, calutrons bend a beam of ions to separate and collect U-235. Because U-235 atoms are lighter, they respond more readily than U-238 to the magnetic push, facilitating the separation.

The second type of fissionable material is PU-239. This material, though not a natural element, is easily produced by uranium-powered nuclear reactors. As a testament to the possibility of developing nuclear weapons with PU-239, all five of the original nuclear powers employed this process in their respective programs, as have both Israel and India (Mazarr 1995, 35-40).

The next step in producing a nuclear device requires the ability to split or fission atoms-- the need for a detonator. Currently employed are two methods--the gun-type design and the implosion detonator. Of the two fissionable materials U-235 and PU-239, U-235, because of its slow chain reaction time, is the easiest substance to explode. The gun-type explosive trigger (uranium detonator), a simple design type, brings two fissile matters together at sufficient speed to create a chain reaction. PU-239, a more difficult substance to handle, requires an implosion detonator to induce a chain reaction.

By 1991, Iraq had successfully employed three techniques for producing uranium-235: EMIS using calutrons, chemical enrichment, and gaseous-centrifuge enrichment (Ekeus 1991, 4). In light of this discovery, in 1991, Joseph Bermudez, a military analyst, stated, "If North Korea's nuclear program is following the Iraq model (U-235), it apparently possesses the scientific, technological and industrial capacity to currently produce a small crude, enriched uranium bomb" (Mazarr 1995, 42-43).

On 20 October 1993, under the supervision of the Nuclear-Chemical Defense Bureau, a plutonium triggering device and PU-238 was exploded in the mountains at Yomsogol (see figure 1). According to another version, the experiment exploded a mock experimental bomb to observe its explosive sound, the flash of light, heat, and the formation of a mushroom cloud (Pike 2001).

From the Nonproliferation Treaty to the Agreed Framework

Signing of the Nonproliferation Treaty

Though North Korea joined the IAEA in 1974, it took more than a decade before it agreed to sign the NPT, in December 1985 (see appendix G for full text of treaty). Concurrent with the signing of the NPT, North Korea sought Soviet assistance in expanding its nuclear energy program. Consequently, this need for assistance proved to be the vehicle that permitted the Soviets to coerce the North Koreans into signing the NPT. In accordance with the treaty, signatories had eighteen months in which to sign the IAEA full-scope safeguards agreement, a contract that authorized the IAEA to conduct both announced and unannounced inspections of all declared nuclear reactors. These inspections are designed to prevent treaty signatories from diverting plutonium for weapons production. On 12 December, in the city of Moscow, Korean Workers' Party Secretary Kang Son San, on behalf of the North Korean government, signed the NPT. However, instead of providing North Korea with a type 153-general inspection form, the IAEA, incorrectly issued them a type 66-agreement form, an individual site declaration form. After not recognizing their mistake for eighteen months, in June 1987, the IAEA reissued North Korea the proper form, allowing North Korea another eighteen months to submit the completed form. Notwithstanding an unprecedented thirty-six months in which to enter a full-scope agreement, December 1988 passed without North Korea signing the inspection form. It took yet

18

another three years before Pyongyang finally yielded to international pressure and signed the IAEA's full-scope safeguards agreement. However, by that time, the full-scope safeguards agreement had expanded beyond declared nuclear sites to include unrestricted access.

United States-North Korea Engagement: A Historic First Meeting

As North Korea stubbornly resisted signing the NPT full-scope safeguards agreement, the US sought multiple methods of inducement to lure North Korea into signing it. On 29 September 1991, following a thirty-five-year deployment of nuclear weapons to South Korea, President Bush signed the Presidential Nuclear Initiative (PNI), ordering the removal of all nuclear weapons from Korea. Then in December of that same year, South Korean President Roh Tae Woo publicly confirmed the removal of all nuclear weapons from South Korea.

While President Bush was carrying out the withdrawal of nuclear weapons from the Korean Peninsula, President Roh was advocating bilateral relations between South and North Korea. As a result, on 20 January 1992, South and North Korea, in an unprecedented action, signed a Joint Declaration of the Denuclearization of the Korean Peninsula (also for brevity referred to as the North-South Joint Declaration) (see appendix A). In short, this agreement pledged that both countries would not "test, manufacture, produce, receive, possess, store, deploy or use nuclear weapons" and would not "possess nuclear reprocessing and uranium enrichment facilities." Moreover, they agreed to reciprocal inspections arranged by a Joint Nuclear Control Commission (Ministry of National Defense 1998, appendix 17).

Three weeks later, on 22 January 1992, the US, represented by Arnold Kanter, the US Under Secretary of State for Political Affairs, and North Korea's Kim Yong Sun, the Korean Workers' Party Secretary for International Relations, met in the highest level contact between the two governments since the signing of the Armistice in 1953. Kanter made two requests: sign the NPT full-scope safeguards agreement and faithfully adhere to the North-South Joint Declaration. Kim counterresponded with his requests: the US needs to stop threatening North Korea, remove

19

all nuclear weapons and military forces from South Korea, and leave the North and South nuclear issues to the Korean people. Additionally, though Kim pushed hard for a follow-up meeting, Kanter refused. On 30 January, in Vienna, Austria, just eight days following the meeting, North Korea signed the IAEA full-scope safeguards agreement. Two months later, on 9 April 1992, in a special meeting of the Supreme People's Assembly, the agreement was ratified and promptly thereafter presented to IAEA Director-General Hans Blix. The following month, on 4 May, North Korea presented the IAEA with a 150-page declaration of its nuclear material and equipment. Among the declarations were three reactors, one radiochemical laboratory (plutonium reprocessing plant), and a disclosure that during the previous year it had reprocessed ninety grams of plutonium.

The Long Awaited Inspections

From 11 to 16 May 1992, Director-General Blix conducted an official visit to North Korea. During his visit, he toured the Yongbyon nuclear research facilities and "reprocessing plant," the 200-megawatt reactor at Taechon, uranium mines in Pakchon and Pyongsan, and research centers in Pyongyang. On 25 May, less than ten days after Director-General Blix's official visit, the first IAEA inspection teams arrived and conducted a rather uneventful series of inspections. Over the next several months, six inspections were conducted.

Through the course of the inspections, the IAEA, through scientific testing, discovered that North Korea was untruthful about its history of plutonium reprocessing. Claiming only to have reprocessed ninety grams of plutonium in 1991, the IAEA inspection teams discovered that North Korea had reprocessed plutonium in 1989, 1990, and 1991.

US intelligence satellite photos provided additional evidence that pinpointed two suspected reprocessed plutonium storage facilities. The IAEA, asserting its new authority to demand special inspections, demanded access to these facilities, but North Korea on repeated occasions refused access based on national sovereignty. During the course of IAEA inspections, the North-South Joint Nuclear Control Commission talks were rapidly deteriorating. North Korea refused unannounced free access to conventional military sites, and the South held firm to its intentions to conduct its annual military exercise--Team Spirit. By March 1993, the North Korean nuclear issue reached crisis proportion. The North Korean government, apparently surprised by the sophistication of the IAEA's inspection capabilities, refused further inspections and submitted a ninety-day notification of intent to withdraw from the NPT.

The next ninety-days were increasingly tense. On 12 May, at the behest of North Korea, US-North Korea working-level meetings were held in Beijing. Because of these meetings, the US and North Korea agreed to hold a second round of high-level talks on 2 June 1993. Representing the US was Robert Gallucci, Assistant Secretary of State for Political-Military Affairs (the future Agreed Framework negotiator). Representing North Korea was Kang Sok Ju, First Vice-Minister of Foreign Affairs. Finally, after a series of four meetings, on 11 June, one day before North Korea's scheduled withdrawal from the NPT, the two sides came to a consensus and signed the first ever US-North Korea joint statement (see appendix B). Though the joint statement defused the immediate threat of Pyongyang's repudiation of the NPT, it failed to resolve the IAEA inspection issue. Breakdown occurred almost immediately following the signing of the joint statement. For months, the IAEA was even denied reentry into the North Korean nuclear facilities to simply service their surveillance cameras (replace batteries and videotapes).

In October 1993, when North Korea finally authorized the IAEA limited access to service their surveillance cameras, the IAEA responded by stating that anything short of full and free access would invalidate inspection continuity, thereby negating all previous inspections. With a growing sense of urgency, the US began pressuring the UN to consider economic and political sanctions against North Korea. Concerned that China might not enforce the sanctions and that North Korea might respond with military force, the US, feeling hamstrung, debated the issue for several months. During this period, the US showed signs of policy wavering. Initially firm on its stance of no nuclear weapons in North Korea, in 1994, Secretary of Defense William Perry stated, "Our policy right along [in Korea] has been oriented to try to keep North Korea from getting a significant nuclear-weapon capability." Of the single bomb risk, Perry stated, "We don't know anything we can do about that. What we can do something about, though, is stopping them from building beyond that" (Mazarr 1995, 150).

In May 1994, North Korea reported their intentions of refueling the main Yongbyon reactor. The reactor, fueled by 8,000 fuel rods, held enough plutonium to build four or five nuclear warheads (Mazarr 1995, 157). Hans Blix, IAEA Director-General, demanded that his team be present for the refueling and be permitted to conduct samplings in order to determine past defueling operations. North Korea refused to agree to this request.

Jimmy Carter: National Security Emissary

As the US rallied support for UN sanctions, Jimmy Carter was dispatched to Pyongyang where he met with Kim Il Sung in an eleventh-hour attempt to make it unnecessary for the US to launch what appeared to many as an inevitable preemptive military strike against the Yongbyon nuclear reactor complex. On 15 June 1994, as Carter visited Kim Il Sung, a *Wall Street Journal* column written by Karen Elliott House exemplified the thoughts of numerous observers:

> Nevertheless we now have the spectacle of global arbitrator Jimmy Carter, who sought to pull US troops out of South Korea during his presidency, traipsing off to Pyongyang when President Clinton ought to be sending Norman Schwarzkopf--perhaps with a few sample photos of high-tech warfare in the Gulf. The emissary's message: Here's what we will do for you [diplomatic relations, aid] if you abandon nuclear ambitions; here's what we will do to you if you don't. The administration has to be willing not only to go to war on the Korean Peninsula but also to put the US-China relationship on the line. . . .[I]t must tell Beijing privately that the US is prepared to sink any Chinese ship that approaches North Korea and bomb any Chinese transport as soon as it crosses the border into North Korea. (*Wall Street Journal* 15 June 1994, A-19)

On the same day, the *Washington Post* carried columns by former Bush administration officials National Security Adviser Brent Scowcroft and Under Secretary of State Arnold Kanter advocating much of the same position.

In Pyongyang, Carter secured from Kim Il Sung a commitment to freeze his nuclear weapons program and to accept IAEA inspectors. Additionally, Carter told Kim that the US had halted its efforts to rally UN sanctions against North Korea, an untrue statement that infuriated the Clinton administration. Finally, because of Carter's visit, both nations stepped back from the brink of war, and Kim Il Sung agreed to meet with South Korean President Kim Young Sam. However, before the meeting could be held, the eighty-four-year-old Kim Il Sung unexpectedly died.

The Agreed Framework: Framing, Pros and Cons, and Korean Peninsula Energy Development Organization Implementation Efforts

Gallucci and Kang: Framers of the Agreed Framework

On 21 June 1994, Ambassador-at-Large Robert Gallucci sent a letter to First Vice-Minister of Foreign Affairs Kang Sok Ju, requesting a third round of high-level talks. North Korea accepted and the date was set for 8 July. However, Kim Il Sung died of a sudden heart attack on that very day, and the talks were delayed until after the funeral. High-level talks recommenced on 5 August, and on 12 August 1994 the two sides, having agreed to a few basic commitments, signed the Agreed Statement between the United States and the Democratic People's Republic of Korea (for full text see appendix C):

> The DPRK is prepared to replace its graphite-moderated reactors and related facilities with light-water reactor (LWR) power plants, and the US is prepared to make arrangements for the provision of LWRs of approximately 2,000 megawatts to the DPRK as early as possible. Upon receipt of US assurance for the provision of LWRs and for arrangements for interim energy alternatives, the DPRK will freeze construction of the 50-megawatt and 200-megawatt reactors, forgo reprocessing, and seal the Radiochemical Laboratory, to be monitored by the IAEA.

From 10 to 29 September, during the high-level talks, Gallucci informed Kang that Seoul would have to play the primary role in the construction of LWRs. Kang rejected this approach and returned to Pyongyang. The rejection proved to be short lived, and within a month the talks resumed in Geneva. Using the 12 August 1994 Agreed Statement as a foundation, the two sides

23

crafted a final accord titled the Agreed Framework between the US and North Korea, dated 21

October 1994 (see appendixes D and E).

Concessions and Compromises:
Contractual Clauses of the Agreed Framework

The Agreed Framework is not a treaty; rather it is an accord that obligates both the US

and North Korea to fulfill reciprocal requirements. The Agreed Framework, divided into four

distinct articles, is summarized in the following paragraphs.

Article One committed both sides to cooperate in the replacement of North Korea's

graphite-moderated nuclear reactors and related facilities with LWR power plants. Specifically,

the US agreed to the following: (1) coordinate the construction of a 2000-megawatt capacity

LWR project, which would be completed by the year 2003, (2) organize an international

consortium to finance and supply the LWR project to be provided to North Korea and serve as the

primary point of contact of this consortium, and (3) secure the conclusion of a supply contract for

the project by 21 April 1995. Finally, as necessary, the US and North Korea were to conclude a

bilateral agreement for the cooperation in the field of peaceful uses of nuclear energy, the US,

representing the consortium, was to provide North Korea, pending completion of the first LWR

unit, 500,000 metric tons of heavy oil per annum for heating and electricity production.

North Korea agreed to freeze and eventually dismantle its graphite-moderated reactors

and related facilities upon receipt of US assurance of the provision of LWRs and for arrangement

of annual shipments of heavy fuel oil. Additionally, in accordance with Article One, North Korea

agreed to the following: (1) by 21 November 1994, North Korea would freeze its graphite-

moderated reactors and permit the IAEA to monitor the entire freeze process; and (2) upon

completion of the LWR project, North Korea would completely dismantle its graphite-moderated

reactors and related facilities.

Finally, Article One committed both countries to the following: (1) During the

construction of the LWR, the US and North Korea were to cooperate in safe storage and disposal

24

of the spent fuel from North Korea's five-megawatt reactor. (2) As soon as possible after the signing of the Agreed Framework, both parties were to hold two sets of expert talks in order to address the specific requirements associated with the LWR program, heavy fuel oil delivery, and the storage and disposal of the spent nuclear fuel rods.

Article Two contained a progressive formula for integrating North Korea into the international community. Specifically, both sides agreed that by January 1995 they would reduce barriers to trade and investment, including restrictions on telecommunications services and financial transactions. Each side agreed that, following the resolution of consular and other technical issues, they would reciprocally open capital-city liaison offices. Finally, as progress was made on "issues concerning each side," liaison offices were to be upgraded to the ambassadorial level.

Article Three directed that a joint effort be made toward establishing peace and security on a nuclear-free Korean Peninsula. North Korea's perpetual anxieties over a US-initiated nuclear weapons attack were to be eased by the US renouncing the use of nuclear weapons on the Korean Peninsula. In exchange, North Korea made a commitment to take steps towards implementing the North-South Joint Declaration on the Denuclearization of the Korean Peninsula. In this joint pledge North and South Korea had agreed to prohibit the manufacture, possession, storage, or acquisition of nuclear weapons, and their ability to reprocess nuclear material. Finally, inasmuch as the Agreed Framework was designed to encourage international dialogue, North Korea agreed to engage in a North-South dialogue.

Article Four committed both sides to work together to strengthen the international nuclear nonproliferation regime. Specifically, North Korea agreed to remain a party to the NPT and to allow implementation of its safeguards agreement. Upon conclusion of the LWR supply contract, IAEA safeguards agreement inspections, both ad hoc and routine, were to resume with respect to the facilities not subject to the freeze. When a significant portion of the LWR project was completed, but before delivery of essential nuclear components, North Korea was to come into full compliance with its safeguards agreement with the IAEA.

Korean Peninsula Energy Development Organization, the Key to the Process

The Agreed Framework obligated the US and North Korea to hold two sets of technical talks. The first set of talks, held in Pyongyang on 24 January 1995, ended in an agreement to place the spent fuel rods from Yongbyon Reactor-2 into dry storage. Then on 16 May 1995, the US and North Korea held the second set of technical talks in Kuala Lumpur. Their purpose was to negotiate the transfer of the LWRs and an interim energy source, compensating North Korea for freezing their nuclear energy program. Though North Korea at first protested vehemently over the suggestion that South Korea provide the nuclear reactors, it eventually acquiesced when it realized that no other country was willing to absorb the cost[1] and risk associated with building the LWRs. Finally, on 12 June 1995, a joint statement was signed acknowledging that a multinational consortium called the Korean Peninsula Energy Development Organization (KEDO)[2] would supply the agreed upon material to North Korea.

KEDO was established on 15 March 1995, when Japan, South Korea, and the US expressed their common desire to advance the implementation of the key provisions of the Agreed Framework and signed KEDO's charter. As KEDO's founding members, these three countries constituted the Organization's Executive Board. KEDO performs four principal functions: (1) promotes nuclear nonproliferation norms, (2) encourages indirect South-North dialogue, (3) promotes constructive engagement between the US and North Korea, and (4) coordinates US policy with Japan and South Korea (Wit 1999, 61). On 30 May 1995, Finland became a member of KEDO by accepting the principles within the organization's charter. Later in 1995, New Zealand, Australia, and Canada joined Finland as members of KEDO. On 15 December 1995, fourteen months after the signing of the Agreed Framework and eight months after the date stipulated in the Agreed Framework for signing a supply contract, KEDO completed its first significant accomplishment, the joint signing of the *Reactor Supply Agreement* with North Korea (see appendix F).

In 1996 Indonesia, Chile , and Argentina joined the Organization. On 19 September 1997, the European Atomic Energy Community joined KEDO with representation on the KEDO Executive Board for a term to coincide with their substantial and sustained support. Later that year the Republic of Poland joined and in 1999, the Czech Republic became KEDO's thirteenth member. In addition to contributions from its member states, KEDO has also received material and financial support from sixteen other nonmember states.

Promoting Nuclear Nonproliferation Norms. Central among KEDO's responsibilities is the promotion of nuclear nonproliferation norms, both international and regional. North Korea is supposedly bound to regional nonproliferation by conditions of the North-South Joint Declaration on the Denuclearization of the Korean Peninsula, as stipulated in Article III of the Agreed Framework. North Korea is also obligated to international nonproliferation by the IAEA NPT, as stipulated in Article IV of the Agreed Framework. Before transfer of essential nuclear components for the LWR, North Korea must, once again, become a full member of the NPT, by submitting to full-scope safeguards inspections by the IAEA.

Encouraging Indirect South-North Dialogue. An important purpose for creating KEDO was to provide an environment that both necessitates and facilitates positive dialogue and opportunities to develop relationships of trust. The opportunities presented for literally thousands of South and North Koreans to work together peacefully extends from the executive level all the way down to construction workers at the nuclear reactor site.

Promote Constructive Engagement between the US and North Korea. Rather than pursuing a policy of containment, the US adopted an approach that could build a relationship of trust and provide a mechanism for constructive engagement. There are two principal objectives of this engagement. The first is a systematic process of modernization that rises from the efforts of

27

the LWR project. This multibillion-dollar project provides the impetus for introducing Western forms of safety, construction, and business practices to North Korea and hopefully will serve as a paradigm for future engagement opportunities. The second goal is that KEDO will serve as an organizational framework for ending North Korea's reclusive and bellicose behavior and for making it an active and positive participant in both regional and international relations.

Harmonization of National Policies. Understandably, the US, South Korean, and Japanese governments each have their own agendas and interests in regard to resolving the North Korean nuclear issue. Therein lies the necessity of KEDO, a forum that facilitates the "harmonizing" of national interests. Board members meet, present their governments' position on specific issues, and then, through a process of protocol revisions, develop a synthesized agreement that is presented for consideration to North Korea.

This summarization of the key issues relevant to the Agreed Framework demonstrates the need for the US to have an adequate policy plan for the denuclearization of North Korea. The next chapter defines the research methodology used in this study. Specifically, it outlines four possible policy options for eliminating a North Korean nuclear weapons threat, and defines the evaluation criteria used to determine the advantages and disadvantages of each option.

---

[1] The cost of the project is earmarked between $4 and $5 billion and will be financed as indicated: South Korea--$3.22 billion, Japan--$1 billion, the European Union--$130 million, and the United States--$55 million (Korea Herald [Seoul] 9 June 1998).

[2] KEDO, an international organization, like the United Nations, has certain state privileges, among which include the issuing of KEDO diplomatic passports, which facilitates the movement of workers through North Korea.

CHAPTER 3

RESEARCH METHODOLOGY

The purpose of this study is to assess the Agreed Framework and other possible options

for ending North Korea's nuclear weapons program. Chapter 2 presented the historical events that

led to the signing of the Agreed Framework. It also described some of the results of this

agreement, including the establishment of KEDO. This chapter lays out four policy options for

addressing the North Korean nuclear weapons issue and the national security objectives that these

four options must achieve. The four policy options are: (1) maintain the status quo of the Agreed

Framework, (2) amend the Agreed Framework, (3) connect other security issues to the Agreed

Framework, or (4) employ economic and military power to force the denuclearization of North

Korea. The three national security objectives are: (1) promoting the nuclear nonproliferation

regime; (2) enhancing the security of allies; and (3) maintaining the US influence in Northeast

Asia (Clinton 2000, 4-9). This chapter then shows how the FAS (feasibility, acceptability, and

suitability) test will be used to analyze each policy option as a way to achieve the permanent or

long-term denuclearization of North Korea.

Strategic planners, in evaluating policy options, often use the three criteria of feasibility,

acceptability, and suitability. They makeup what is commonly referred to as a FAS test. These

terms are defined in Joint Publication 1-02, the *Department of Defense Dictionary of Military and

Associated Terms*, as follows (United States Department of Defense 2000):

> Feasibility--The determination of whether the assigned tasks could be accomplished by using available resources. (170)
>
> Acceptability--The determination whether the contemplated course of action is worth the cost in manpower, material, and time involved; is consistent with the law of war; and militarily and politically supportable. (1)
>
> Suitability--The determination that the course of action will reasonably accomplish the identified objectives, missions, or tasks if carried out successfully. (443)

Taken together, these criteria provide the framework used in this study to determine the best

course of action for achieving the verifiable end of North Korea's nuclear weapons program.

United States Objectives in Northeast Asia

The US security objectives in Northeast Asia, as extracted from the *National Security Strategy*, include: (1) promoting the nuclear nonproliferation regime, (2) enhancing the security of US allies, and (3) maintaining the influence of the US in Northeast Asia (Clinton 2000, 4-9). Bringing an end to the North Korean nuclear weapons program is an important element in achieving these three objectives. Policies and courses of action designed to eliminate North Korea's nuclear weapons program that adversely affect efforts to achieve other objectives may not be acceptable or suitable even if they are feasible. By examining the feasibility, acceptability, and suitability of each policy option, this study seeks to determine the potential utility of each policy option in achieving *National Security Strategy* objectives. The goal is to help clarify the debate about what policies and actions can best contribute to resolving North Korea's nuclear challenge to US national security.

National Security Objectives

Promote the Nuclear Nonproliferation Regime

The nonproliferation of nuclear weapons, as stated in the *National Security Strategy*, is among US vital interests. It is also the overriding objective of the Agreed Framework. Moreover, as stated by the *National Security Strategy*, "The Nonproliferation Treaty, the cornerstone of international nuclear nonproliferation regime, reinforces regional and global security by creating and sustaining confidence in the nonnuclear commitments of its parties" (Clinton 2000, 13). The fostering of international nonproliferation, as stated in the *National Security Strategy*, seeks to ban the international transfer of nuclear weapon components.

It is plausible that North Korea, an economically destitute nation, would find it financially tempting to conduct international nuclear weapons sales, further contributing to the destabilization of global security. An equally dangerous action by North Korea would be its

30

withdrawal from the NPT. Such an action could lead to similar responses by other nations, which could, in turn, lead to the diminution of the international authority of the IAEA.

Among the three critical proliferation zones--the Korean Peninsula, Southwest Asia, and South Asia--North Korea stands foremost in priority (Clinton 2000, 15). The further acquisition of nuclear weapons by North Korea would directly threaten both South Korea and Japan, two US allies in the region. Though military operations on the peninsula could be a destabilizing factor within the region, the US, in order to counter the North Korean military threat, must retain the freedom to employ its military instrument of power. However, it is plausible to imagine a nuclear powered North Korea, acting as a regional "bully," exacting demands upon its neighbors, while the US stood by in relative impotence. Drawing upon a comparable corollary, Mazarr suggests that had Iraq possessed nuclear weapons during the Gulf War, the US response might have been significantly different (Mazarr 1995, 219). Of equal or greater concern is the possible regional nuclear arms race that could ensue. Such an arms race could lead to the development of nuclear weapons by South Korea, Japan, or Taiwan.

Enhance the Security of Allies

As stated in the *National Security Strategy*, among US vital interests is the physical security of its allies (Clinton 2000, 4). Consequently, any military action that the US would contemplate in this region must be conducted in the multilateral arena, particularly, in close cooperation with both Japan and South Korea. Actions that would provoke a war in South Korea or Japan should be avoided. Additionally, actions that would destabilize the region in such a manner as to disrupt the economic vitality of both South Korea and Japan must be avoided. Undisputedly, a major theater war fought on the Korean Peninsula would economically devastate Northeast Asia, as much of its infrastructure would likely be destroyed and the flow of trade interrupted. Japan, the world's second largest economy, exports a staggering $120 billion to the US annually and imports one-half that amount from the US alone. Similarly, South Korea is the

31

world's eleventh largest economy, a major world economic leader whose absence from the international market, as would likely occur if war broke out on the peninsula, would have far-reaching global effects.

Maintain United States Influence in Northeast Asia

The pursuit of national interests requires international engagement, both as a member of international organizations and as an autonomous state actor. The denuclearization of North Korea, as well as any other regional issue, requires the US to consider other regional actors, both allied and opposed. Failure to do so could result in abrasive relations and policy failures. The *National Security Strategy* states that an important national interest is the ability to influence regional events in Northeast Asia (Clinton 2000, 9). The ability of the US to pursue its interests in this region is predicated, to a large extent, on its associations with the nations in this region (South Korea, Japan, China, Russia, and North Korea). Among these five nations, US relationships with South Korea and Japan are paramount. United States defense treaties with South Korea and Japan allow the forward deploying of military forces in both countries. If forward presence and the strength of these alliances are to be maintained, the US will need to perpetuate its credibility as a responsible partner. Therefore, its efforts to stop North Korea from developing nuclear weapons, particularly any actions that might adversely affect the vital interests (physical and economic security) of allies, must be mutually approved.

Policy Options for Denuclearizing North Korea

The Status Quo Option--Agreed Framework

The Agreed Framework is neither a treaty nor a legally binding contract. Its purpose is to facilitate the mutual progress of both the US and North Korea through a series of quid pro quo agreements. For the US, the overarching purpose of this agreement is to eliminate North Korea's ability to manufacture nuclear weapons (denuclearization). For North Korea, the principal objectives are to obtain LWR technology and to establish diplomatic and economic relations with the US. Although there would be no legal ramifications were the US to either alter or abandon the Agreed Framework, any action taken without the consent of North Korea would likely result in a breach of trust, undermining both this agreement and the ability to negotiate any future agreement. The analysis of this policy option centers on obstacles that might prohibit the completion of the Agreed Framework, where such obstacles may exist, possible options that would not require an amendment to the Agreed Framework, or those that might will be considered.

The Amended Framework Option

Since the Agreed Framework is only a means to achieve a policy objective and not the objective itself, there is no restriction to negotiating necessary changes. Consequently, if the Agreed Framework, as written, is flawed or otherwise incompatible with the US intended policy objective--the permanent or long-term denuclearization of North Korea--then the agreement should either be amended or dissolved.

A reoccurring concern by experts who have analyzed the Agreed Framework is the inability of North Korea to distribute the energy that the LWRs will produce. The basis for this argument is the decrepit state of North Korea's power grid network. Consequently, recurring debates have surfaced as how best to resolve this obstacle. The US position in this matter, as stated by the State Department, is, "We have no intention of agreeing to [any] add-ons which are outside of the normal scope [of a LWR] or which would significantly increase the cost of the project" (Sigal 1998, 201). However, some critics, including the Nautilus Institute,[1] contend that improving the North Korea power grid is in the interest of the US, and they therefore recommend amending the Agreed Framework to facilitate such a project (Von Hippel and Hayes 2001, 18).

Because North Korea's capacity to use LWRs is uncertain, as part of the amended framework option, its energy sector will be analyzed. The Nautilus Institute's proposed amendment to the Agreed Framework will also be analyzed and its potential for achieving the goals of the Agreed Framework will be assessed.

The Comprehensive Framework Option

Whereas an amended framework could be used to resolve obstacles blocking the completion of the Agreed Framework, the adoption of a comprehensive framework is another possible policy option. A comprehensive framework would capture critical security issues that were not included in the Agreed Framework. Since the signing of the Agreed Framework in 1994, the US has unilaterally attached many conditions to it.

The first condition was attached in 1999, following a presidential policy review of US-North Korea relations. This policy review, conducted by Dr. William J. Perry, connected the normalization of US-North Korea relations to two requirements: North Korea's verifiable elimination of its nuclear weapons program and its long-range missile program.

Other conditions followed. In June 2001, Washington predicated reopening US-North Korea talks on Pyongyang's willingness to discuss three important issues: the elimination of North Korea's nuclear weapon and missile programs and the reduction of its conventional force (*New York Times* 7 June 2001). By November, Washington added the elimination of Pyongyang's chemical and biological weapons program to its agenda (*New York Times* 26 November 2001).

Because of the central role of missiles in delivering nuclear payloads, the discussion of the comprehensive framework option will contain an analysis of the threat of North Korea's ballistic missile program. Concurrently, an analysis will be conducted of Dr. Perry's *Review of United States Policy toward North Korea: Findings and Recommendations* to determine the ability of the comprehensive framework option to achieve the permanent or long-term denuclearization of North Korea.

The Coercive Denuclearization Option

Coercive denuclearization would apply force until North Korea agreed to abandon its nuclear program. Critical to this policy option is the proper identification of North Korea's pain threshold, followed by a relentless application of proper force. Economic sanctions, military actions, or a combination of both would be the primary focus of this policy option.

On 19 March 1993, Frank Gaffney, President of the Center for Security Policy, wrote a decision brief titled *What to do about North Korea's Nuclear Threat: Execute the 'Osirak' Remedy.* In short, Gaffney recommend that following a US military buildup on the Korean Peninsula, the US should demand that IAEA inspectors be given prompt unfettered access to all suspected North Korean nuclear weapons related activities. If the ultimatum were defied, the US, following the precedence of the Israeli strike upon Osirak-1, an Iraqi nuclear power reactor, would then immediately conduct preemptive strikes upon selected North Korean nuclear weapons program sites. Fifteen months later, Senator John McCain (Republican-Arizona), in a speech to the US Senate (US Congress 1994), recommended a policy option for denuclearizing North Korean that closely paralleled Gaffney's recommendation. The recommendations of Frank Gaffney and Senator McCain, both focusing upon preemptive counterproliferation (PCP) and economic sanctions, encompass and define what this study calls coercive denuclearization.

The research methodology detailed in this chapter will be used in the next chapter to evaluate the benefits and drawbacks of each policy option with regards to achieving the permanent or long-term denuclearization of North Korea. The FAS test is the tool that is used for conducting the analysis of each policy option.

---

[1]Nautilus Institute is a nonprofit organization based in Berkeley, CA. The Institute's mission is to solve interrelated critical global problems by improving the processes and outcomes of global governance. The Nautilus Institute's Energy, Security and Environment Program, started in 1996, analyzes the nexus of energy, security, and environmental issues in Northeast Asia. Based on this analysis policy initiatives are developed. The twin fields of "environmental security" and "energy security," as applied in Northeast Asia, underlie much of the work of the program.

CHAPTER 4

ANALYSIS

As stated in the preceding chapter, the US has three prominent national security

objectives in Northeast Asia, namely, to promote the nonproliferation regime, to enhance the

security of allies, and to maintain US influence in the region, but as far as North Korea is

concerned there is clearly one major objective--the permanent or long-term denuclearization of

North Korea. The previous chapter discussed four possible policy options that might achieve this

objective. They are: (1) continuing with the Agreed Framework, (2) amending the Agreed

Framework, (3) adopting a more comprehensive framework, and (4) undertaking a coercive

denuclearization option. This chapter analyzes these various options to determine their value as

ways to achieve North Korean denuclearization, while allowing the US to pursue successfully its

other two national security goals in Northeast Asia. The FAS test is the method at the heart of this

analysis.

The Status Quo Option--The Agreed Framework

The status quo option is the Agreed Framework, the analysis of which includes a look at

the original assumptions under which it was written. On 13 December 2001, the author asked

Ambassador Thomas C. Hubbard if the Agreed Framework was achieving its intended purpose.

He stated, "The Agreed Framework was designed to freeze North Korea's existing nuclear

program, and it has done that." He went on to discuss how there are yet a number of unresolved

issues, such as IAEA inspections, dismantling of the nuclear reactors, and the relinquishing of the

canned fuel rods (Hubbard 2001). In line with Ambassador Hubbard's statement, it is important

to understand that when the Clinton administration wrote the Agreed Framework, it was only

intended to address the nuclear weapons proliferation issue as it applied to North Korea.

Specifically, the immediate focus of the agreement was the elimination of Pyongyang's weapons-

grade plutonium production capability, which was to be followed by North Korea's recommitment to the NPT. Reembracing this treaty would also precipitate the renewal of IAEA led full-scope safeguards inspection, a process that would verify North Korea's holdings of weapons-grade plutonium (PU-239) and ensure the cessation of all nuclear weapons production capabilities. Additionally, the Agreed Framework obligated Pyongyang to commit to the North-South Joint Declaration on the Denuclearization of the Korean Peninsula and to begin an era of reciprocity with South Korea.

Planning Assumptions for the Agreed Framework

Larry Niksch, Asian Affairs Specialist for the US Congressional Research Service, in 1995 identified three assumptions that the Clinton administration used when developing the Agreed Framework. In a paper prepared for the International Workshop on the US-South Korea Alliance, Niksch stated the following:

> Behind the Administration's [Agreed Framework] policy lies a layer of assumptions concerning North Korea's motivations and its future. One assumption emphasizes the defensive nature of North Korea's actions. Pyongyang, it is argued, acts out of fear of being dominated by South Korea even when it commits egregious acts. . . .
> Another set of assumptions stresses the inevitability of future change in North Korea. Such change, Administration and State Department officials believe, will improve the security situation on the Korean Peninsula and will render relatively unimportant the questions of North Korea's past plutonium and atomic bomb production and the implementation of Pyongyang's obligations related to inspections, fuel rod removal, and dismantlement of nuclear installations. [This] set of assumptions stresses the inevitability or high likelihood of North Korea instituting economic reforms and opening up to the outside world. . . .
> The third variation is the most far reaching: the North Korean regime faces a certain collapse and will be replaced by a more reasonable successor. . . . (1995, 8-9)

The first assumption, that North Korea fears domination by South Korea, may have been manifested and affirmed in North Korea's attempts to diplomatically isolate South Korea.[2] Some recent examples include a North Korean effort to weaken the mechanisms of the Korean armistice agreement and to pressure the US to sign a bilateral peace agreement. It could be argued that the Agreed Framework, a bilateral accord with heavy three-party responsibilities, should have been a multilateral agreement including South Korea as a third party. Fear of domination may have also motivated Pyongyang's refusal to sign the reactor supply contract until, the term "South Korean standard reactor" was eliminated from the contract (Sigal 1998, 201). A less benign interpretation of North Korea actions is not that it fears South Korea domination, but seeks itself to dominate relations and assert its authority over the peninsula.

The second and third Clinton administration assumptions are even more open to question. Both anticipate a regime change that would lead to economic and political reforms. Looking at these assumptions eight years after the Agreed Framework was signed, both of them seem to be invalid. First, the death of Kim Il Sung in 1994 was not the catalyst for much change, and it did not lead to a disintegration of the North Korean government. Rather, it simply initiated the nation's first, peaceful transition of national power. Second, North Korea, rather than opening its economy to the world, has become a "beggar nation." Third, North Korea shows few signs of becoming a responsible member of the international community.

Because the planning assumptions have yet to be validated, it is plausible to infer that the Agreed Framework, as a policy option, is a questionable or weak way to achieve the US main policy objective--the permanent or long-term denuclearization of North Korea. In fact, this analysis suggests that the Agreed Framework cannot be fully implemented and thus cannot achieve its main objective. In particular, it appears impossible for the US to do what the Agreed Framework commits it to do. If the assumptions underlying an agreement have been shown to be false, and the agreement itself cannot be implemented, there is reason to question continued reliance on that agreement as a way to achieve the policy objectives it was originally designed to reach. The findings are articulated in the next several paragraphs.

Elimination of North Korea's Nuclear Weapons

Articles One, Three, and Four of the Agreed Framework are specifically designed to achieve the critical policy objective of eliminating North Korea's nuclear weapons program. Article One has a short-term focus, emphasizing first the freezing of specified nuclear reactors and facilities followed by their eventual dismantling. Article Four takes the long-term approach by eliminating North Korea's nuclear weapons program through comprehensive IAEA full-scope safeguards inspections. Article Three of the Agreed Framework calls for "both sides to work together for peace and security on a nuclear-free Korean Peninsula," which includes "steps to implement the North-South Joint Declaration on the Denuclearization of the Korean Peninsula." This Joint Declaration, which was made in January 1992, was more stringent than the IAEA safeguard requirements. It contained a commitment by both North and South Korea not to manufacture, possess, store, or acquire nuclear weapons, and it also prohibited either side from having nuclear reprocessing or uranium enrichment facilities. However, since late 1992, the North-South Joint Declaration has been dormant because of Joint Declaration related disputes that resulted in the cancellation of inspections by the Joint Nuclear Control Committee (Mazarr 1995, 87).

As indicated in chapter 2, many factors have delayed the implementation of the Agreed Framework, one of which was North Korea's initial rejection of the Korean Electric Power Company (KEPCO) as the LWR contractor. Further complications have delayed the LWR program to the point where construction on the first reactor building is not even scheduled to begin until August 2002 (Vogelaar 2001, 1), eight full years after the signing of the agreement.

In addition to problems constructing the LWRs, KEDO has also faced hurdles in delivering the agreed 500,000 tons of HFO per annum to North Korea. Since the beginning, this task has been plagued by funding resistance from the US Congress. In accordance with the Agreed Framework, the US has the principal responsibility for paying for this oil, and, given the size of the US federal budget, these expenditures constitute a relatively small amount of money. However, because Congress is skeptical of the Agreed Framework and considers it a form of appeasement, it has delayed funding for nearly every shipment. Increases in the cost of HFO have also added to Congress' disdain of the Agreed Framework. Congressional unhappiness is sure to increase in the future because the cost of safely storing, shipping and disposing of North Korea's spent fuel rods, and dismantling North Korea's existing nuclear facilities will likely bring total US expenditures under the Agreed Framework to more than $1 billion (Wit 1999, 67).

Another set of problems has to do with inspections. Despite the spent fuel rods at Yongbyon having been canned, they have yet to be inspected or disposed of properly. The dismantling of the frozen reactors and facilities are contingent on the completed construction of the first LWR. Completion was originally planned for 2003, but various project delays have precluded the LWRs from being completed until no earlier than 2009 (*Tokyo Shimbum* [Daily News] 29 December 2001). Finally, the long-term assurance of North Korea's cessation of its nuclear weapons program requires the IAEA to complete its comprehensive full-scope safeguards inspections. According to the original time line, these inspections were to be completed in 2003 along with the completion of the LWR project, but since these inspections are connected to the completion of the first LWR, these inspections are not likely to be completed any sooner than 2009.

As the IAEA requires three to four years to complete its full-scope safeguards inspections, KEDO has demanded that North Korea allow IAEA inspectors to begin their work now.[3] North Korea is denying access to IAEA inspectors based on the wording of the Agreed Framework, which states that "when a significant portion of the LWR project is completed, but before delivery of key nuclear components, North Korea will come into compliance with its safeguards agreement."[4] From North Korea's perspective, since only preliminary work has been completed, its position is justified under the terms of the *Reactor Supply Agreement* (see appendix F). Besides Pyongyang's right to refuse inspections under the agreement, it is likely that their unwillingness to allow inspections is fed by a fear that "early" compliance with safeguard provisions will leave KEDO with no incentive to complete the project. KEDO, on the other hand, has two worries. The first concern is that billions of dollars will be wasted if the project nears completion and North Korea resists becoming safeguard compliant. The second concern is that if inspections are not initiated soon, there will be a long delay between the completion of the nuclear reactor and delivery of the key nuclear components (Wit 1999, 67), ultimately extending the cost of the overall project (HFO deliveries, construction costs, etc.).[5]

Another obstacle to completing the Agreed Framework is the requirement contained in the reactor supply agreement for North Korea to, "assure that appropriate nuclear regulatory standards and procedures are in place to ensure the safe operation and maintenance of the LWR plants."[6] However, because of the decrepit state of North Korea's power grid, the LWRs could not be operated safely (discussed in depth during the analysis of the amended framework).

Nuclear Regulatory Standards and LWR Transfer Prohibitions

The two nuclear regulatory standards that principally cover the safe operation of the KEDO constructed LWRs are the IAEA Convention on Nuclear Safety (INFCIRC/449), dated 5 July 1994, and the US Nuclear Regulatory Commission Standard Review Plan (NUREG-0800) Revision-3, dated July 1983. The IAEA safety standard requires nations with nuclear reactors to: (1) "establish and maintain a legislative and regulatory framework to govern the safety of nuclear installations," and (2) "establish or designate a regulatory body to enforce the established national safety standards" (International Atomic Energy Agency 2000, 4).

The Nuclear Regulatory Commission safety standard, however, go beyond IAEA measures--it is both descriptive and prescriptive. For example, it mandates that in order to be operated safely a nuclear power plant must be connected to two offsite power systems (also referred to as preferred power systems). Specifically, Nuclear Regulation-0800, chapter 8.2 states the following in regard to the criteria for safety-related electric power systems for nuclear power plants:

> The primary objective . . . of the preferred power system, is to determine that this
> system satisfies the acceptance criteria . . . and will perform its design functions during plant
> normal operation, anticipated operational occurrences, and accident conditions. . . . (4)
> [T]he offsite power system[s] [must have the] capacity and capability to permit functioning of
> structures, systems, and components important to [the nuclear power plant's] safety. . . . The
> preferred power system consists of two physically independent circuits routed from the

41

electrical grid system by transmission lines to the onsite power distribution system. The . . . grid stability [must show] that loss of the largest generating capacity being supplied to the grid . . . will not cause grid instability. . . . (9)
[T]he independence of the two circuits is [so] that both electrical and physical separation exists to minimize the chance of simultaneous failures. . . . (United States Nuclear Regulatory Commission 1983, 1)

According to the Nautilus Institute, North Korea's power grid is too small (Von Hippel and Hayes 2001, 3), regardless of its condition, to safely operate the KEDO reactors without first connecting it to the power grid of a neighboring country (discussed in depth during the analysis of the amended framework).[7] There are also technical issues associated with operating a nuclear reactor on a power grid where frequency fluctuations require the reactor to be shutdown often.[8]

The North Korean power grid is decrepit. Since it has not been fixed, it can be inferred that Pyongyang either lacked or mismanaged its financial resources. Regardless, without repairing the power grid, it is unsafe to operate the LWRs in North Korea. Additionally, the US has stated that it will not assist North Korea in this endeavor.

The final obstacle to the Agreed Framework achieving the denuclearization of North Korea, and the one that appears to have been most dependent upon the aforementioned planning assumptions, is the capability of LWRs (built under the Agreed Framework) to manufacture weapons-grade plutonium. According to an analysis conducted by the Lawrence Livermore National Laboratory, each LWR, in its first fifteen months of normal operation, will produce more than 300 kilograms of weapons-grade plutonium, enough after reprocessing to build sixty implosion warheads (Sokolski 2001, 4). Likewise J. Holdren, in 1989, reported that in one year a one-gigawatt (1,000-megawatt) LWR could produce between 200 and 250 kilograms of reactor-grade plutonium, enough for at least thirty to forty bombs[9] (1989, 174). There are, however, according to the Council for Nuclear Fuel Cycle at the Institute for Energy Economics in Japan, certain factors that complicate creating nuclear bombs with reactor-grade plutonium, which are:

The use of reactor-grade plutonium complicates [nuclear] bomb design for several reasons. First and most important, Pu-240 has a high rate of spontaneous fission, meaning that the plutonium in the device will continually produce many background neutrons. Second, the isotope Pu-238 decays relatively rapidly, thereby significantly increasing the rate of heat generation in the material. Third the isotope Americium (Am) 241 (which results from the 14-year half-life decay of Pu-241) emits highly penetrating gamma rays, increasing the radioactive exposure of any personnel handling the material. (Council for Nuclear Fuel Cycle, Institute for Energy Economics, Japan 2001, 6)

Notwithstanding the challenges presented by these additional isotopes, the aforementioned institution and others, like the Committee on International Security and Arms Control of the National Academy of Sciences, and J. Carson Mark, former director of the Theoretical Division at Los Alamos National Laboratory from 1947 to 1972, have stated that it is not appreciably more difficult to design a weapon using reactor-grade plutonium vice weapons-grade plutonium.[10] In addressing the aforementioned challenges, the Committee on International Security and Arms Control of the National Academy of Sciences stated the following:

> [Although] Pu-240 will set off the reaction prematurely. . . . Calculations demonstrate, however, that even if pre-initiation occurs at the worst possible moment (when the material first becomes compressed enough to sustain a chain reaction), the explosive yield of even a relatively simple device similar to the Nagasaki bomb would be of the order of one or a few kilotons.[11] Regardless of how high the concentration of troublesome isotopes is, the yield would not be less. With a more sophisticated design, weapons could be built with reactor-grade plutonium that would be assured of having higher yields. . . .
>
> The heat generated by Pu-238 and Pu-240 requires careful management of the heat in the device. Means to address this problem include providing channels to conduct the heat from the plutonium through the insulating explosive surrounding the core, or delaying assembly of the device until a few minutes before it is to be used. . . .
>
> The radiation from Americuim-241 means that more shielding and greater precautions to protect personnel might be necessary when building and handling nuclear explosives made from reactor-grade plutonium. But these difficulties are not prohibitive. (Committee on International Security and Arms Control of the National Academy of Sciences 1994, 33)

If such opinions are valid, coupled with North Korea's past resistance to various inspection regimes, it does not require much analysis to hypothesize a situation where, following the transfer of the LWRs, North Korea could expel the IAEA inspectors and then operate the LWRs (for up to three years without refueling) for the distinct purpose of creating nuclear weapons. If such a scenario were to occur, adherence to the Agreed Framework would not only have brought harm to the long-term regional security of Northeast Asia, it also would have created a more volatile situation than the one that induced the crisis of 1994 and led to the signing of the Agreed Framework in the first place.

Because of the potential for any nuclear reactor to be misused as a source for producing fissile material, US law prohibits the transfer of nuclear components to unreliable agents. Specifically, the US Atomic Energy Act of 1954, amended in 1978, states the following:

> No nuclear materials and equipment or sensitive nuclear technology shall be exported to (1) any nonnuclear-weapon state that is found by the President to have, at any time after [10 March 1978], (A) detonated a nuclear explosive device; or (B) terminated or abrogated IAEA safeguards; or (C) materially violated an IAEA safeguards agreement; or (D) engaged in activities involving source or special nuclear material and having direct significance for the manufacture or acquisition of nuclear explosive devices, and has failed to take steps which, in the President's judgement, represent sufficient progress toward terminating such activities. (Nuclear Nonproliferation Act 1978, Chap. 11, sec. 129, 138)

North Korea has violated three of the four conditions stipulated by this statute. Though the US President, with Congressional consent, can waive the provisions of this law,[12] it is difficult to imagine either of them doing so, given the fact that the transfer of LWRs to a "hostile" country is paramount to providing it an increased capability to produce nuclear weapons.

Normalization of US-North Korea Relations

Article Two of the Agreed Framework, states that the US and North Korea "will move towards full normalization of political and economic relations." Though small strides have been made, much work has yet to be done in this area. Currently, neither diplomatic relations nor liaison offices have been established between the two countries. This is clearly one of the most necessary steps in the entire agreement, yet it continues to be the most neglected.

Since the planning assumption that envisioned the North Korean government becoming more open and reasonable has yet to be validated, continuing to try to implement the Agreed Framework may not be the best approach. But if this agreement is to succeed, actions need to be taken to create the security environment that the assumptions were originally predicated upon. Perhaps, through positive engagement with North Korea, a positive security environment can be created on the Korean Peninsula.

A major initiative to engage North Korea was begun following the inauguration of South Korean President Kim Dae Jung in 1998. This was his so-called "Sunshine Policy" of reaching out to North Korea. The fruits of this policy have been harvested in inter-Korean trade, cultural events, and bilateral visits and talks. The apogee of President Kim's "Sunshine Policy" occurred during a head of state three-day summit, which took place in Pyongyang from 13 to 15 June 2000. This historic event was the impetus for many other significant developments, including the initiation of construction on a trans-peninsula transportation corridor.[13] In addition to the June 2000 Summit, there were inter-Korean Defense Ministerial talks in September of 2000, and other high-level bilateral meetings. In 2001, South Korea provided North Korea with over $120 million in aid (*Joong Ang Ilbo* [Daily News] [Seoul] 5 July 2001); and during this same period, inter-Korean trade reached $402.9 million (*Chosun Ilbo* [Daily news] [Seoul] 9 January 2002).

The good will created by President Kim's "Sunshine Policy" made possible a visit to Pyongyang by Secretary of State Albright in October 2000. There she met with Chairman Kim Jung Il in the highest level meeting yet held between the US and North Korea. An intended, follow-on visit by President Clinton was canceled when the Democratic Party lost the presidential election in November 2000. Following the inauguration of President George W. Bush in January 2001, US-North Korea relations have deteriorated to the near 1994 crisis levels. In late 2001 President Bush repeatedly called upon North Korea to eliminate its weapons of mass destruction (WMD) capabilities. On 29 January 2002, during his State of the Union Address, President Bush identified North Korea, Iraq, and Iran as state sponsors of terror, categorized them as an "axis of evil," and then circuitously threatened preemptive military action against them:

> I will not wait on events, while dangers gather. The United States of America will not permit the world's most dangerous regimes to threaten us with the world's most destructive weapons. . . . We can't stop short. If we stop now--leaving terror camps intact and terror states unchecked--our sense of security would be false and temporary. History has called America and our allies to action, and it is both our responsibility and our privilege to fight freedom's fight. (Bush 2002)

If the success of the Agreed Framework is predicated upon a relationship of trust between Washington and Pyongyang, the worsening of relations between the US and North Korea does not bode well for the Agreed Framework achieving its goals. Perhaps opening capital-city liaison offices could renew the process of building trust in the relationship, a process already conceived of in the Agreed Framework. Movement toward establishing diplomatic relations, and the dual objective of Article Two, the normalization of economic relations with North Korea, a major policy objective of Pyongyang, might also help make the Agreed Framework work. Since 20 January 1988, the US designation of North Korea as a state supporter of terrorism has effectively disqualified North Korea from receiving monetary aid from international financial institutions, like the Asian Development Bank, the World Bank and International Monetary Fund. Additionally, for fifty years, presidents of the US, upholding the Trading with the Enemy Act, have enforced economic sanctions against North Korea. This situation, coupled with such internal problems as irrational central planning, flooding, and drought, has perpetuated North Korea's low gross domestic product, which in 2000 was estimated to be between $16.79 billion (*The Korean Times* 29 April 2002) and $22 billion (Central Intelligence Agency *World Factbook* 2002).

On 19 June 2001, President Bush eased some of the economic sanctions against Pyongyang by permitting American businesses to conduct limited trade with North Korea. This is a start, toward trade normalization, but will probably not have much effect, given North Korea's laws, economic organization, poor products and lack of foreign exchange. Also, few US companies conduct trade with nations that do not have diplomatic relations with the US.

In 2000, North Korea's per capita gross domestic product was $1,000, a drop since 1989 (Central Intelligence Agency 2002). This drop in the North Korean economy was precipitated in part by the collapse of the Warsaw Pact and the Soviet Union between 1989 and 1991. Sixty percent of North Korea's trade in 1989 was with Warsaw Pact countries. Much of that trade was in bartered goods, and the collapse necessitated the use of hard currency after 1991. Heavy flooding in 1995 and 1996 and a drought in 1997, followed by lesser floods and droughts up through this year, have all exacerbated the economic decline. Clearly, North Korea's economy is in trouble.

As a militaristic society and in spite of its economic hardships, North Korea perpetuates a defense budget that consumed, in 1999, 6.2 percent of its gross domestic product, or $1.36 billion (Ministry of National Defense Republic of Korea 2000, 48). To reverse this type of spending is going to take a long-term exposure to a better way, such as a free-market economy, and perhaps some coaxing and cooperation from outside nations, particularly the US, South Korea, Japan, and China.

Some exposure to a better way is beginning to occur on various fronts. As mentioned, high-level bilateral talks between US-North Korea and South Korea-North Korea have occurred. Since January 2000, sixteen nations have established diplomatic relations with North Korea.[14] Additionally, KEDO has become a forum for exposing North Korea to accepted norms of international business practices, while concurrently providing opportunities for thousands of North and South Koreans to work, socialize and to build trust in their relations (Wit 1999, 62). Hence, regardless of the outcome of the Agreed Framework, these experiences will most certainly serve as positive influences for change.

The Status Quo Option--Agreed Framework Evaluated

Feasibility Test: Is Full Implementation of the Agreed Framework Feasible?

For the Agreed Framework to be feasible, the US, its KEDO partners, and North Korea would have to be both willing and able to allocate all required funds necessary to meet each nation's respective obligations. For KEDO, this includes the cost of building the LWRs, delivering HFO, and safely disposing of the 8,000 spent fuel rods from North Korea's five-megawatt GMR. North Korea must repair its power grid so that the LWRs will be able to operate safely, and dismantle its GMRs and their associated facilities.

In 1995, KEDO accepted the financial cost of the Agreed Framework. However, because of the delays in executing the Agreed Framework, the original LWR cost estimates of $4 to $4.5 billion are likely to increase significantly. In 1995, Niksch suggested that as a result of inflation, cost overruns and North Korean requests for a one billion dollar grant to repair its power grid, total project costs could double (Niksch 1995, 2). Already since the signing of the Agreed Framework the US has spent $331 million for KEDO. With the exception of $25.7 million that was spent on canning the fuel rods, nearly all of the money has been used to pay for HFO shipments to North Korea (United States Department of State Congressional Budget 1995 through 2002). Assuming the first LWR is completed in 2009 and the US expenditures to KEDO remain constant with its 2002 payment of $95 million, the cost to the US over the next seven years will be $665 million. Given the large federal budget, it is feasible that the US will be able to meet its financial obligation under the Agreed Framework.

Seoul, however, has yet to decide how to raise $3.22 billion, its share of the $4.5 billion LWR project (*Korea Herald*, [Seoul] 9 June 1998). In 1999, the government issued bonds worth $131 million to fund the preparatory construction, and had planned to raise another $222 million during 2000, though the National Assembly disapproved that plan. If the cost of the LWR project doubles and the percentage of cost sharing remains the same, the South Korean government will have to raise $6.44 billion, a prohibitively expensive cost that is unlikely to be accepted by either South Korean taxpayers or by international capital markets.

North Korea's inane economic system, lack of foreign exchange, and diminutive federal budget impinge on its ability to repair its decrepit power grid, or to build the two independent offsite power circuits that are required by contract for the emergency operation of LWR safety equipment. Consequently, North Korea many not be able to achieve nuclear safety standards of the US and the IAEA, a necessary requirement for the final delivery of the LWRs. Consequently, if North Korea is either unable or unwilling to finance a power grid refurbishment project, it is also unlikely that it would be willing to finance the dismantling of its GMRs and related facilities.

If the cost of the LWR project doubles, it will be infeasible to accomplish the Agreed Framework. Even if one assumes that the cost of the project will not increase substantially, as long as North Korea is held responsible for financing the refurbishment of its power grid, it is plausible to expect that financially it either will not or cannot meet its obligations; therefore, the Agreed Framework is financially infeasible.

Acceptability Test: Is Full Implementation of the Agreed Framework Acceptable to All Parties?

The US and North Korea have shown varying degrees of commitment to the Agreed Framework over the past eight years. North Korea has frozen its GMRs and related facilities, and permitted its spent fuel rods to be canned. The US and KEDO have begun work on the LWR project and have delivered annual shipments of HFO. However, these are only preliminary actions and are insufficient to achieve the denuclearization of North Korea. North Korea's actions are reversible and the US-KEDO actions appear to be delaying tactics. Distrust between the two parties appears to be the roadblock that stalls further progress; notwithstanding, North Korea has extracted residual benefits because of the Agreed Framework that have netted it millions of dollars in international aid and trade. It is uncertain how long these residual benefits alone will continue to pacify North Korea, thereby keeping it from reinitiating its nuclear weapons program.

The Agreed Framework is unacceptable for three reasons: (1) political and economic engagement is currently undesirable; (2) LWRs produce fissile material that can be used to create nuclear weapons; and (3) LWRs cannot safely operate on North Korea's decrepit power grid.

Firstly, as of January 2002, both the US and North Korea appear unwilling to engage. However, this freeze in the relationship has only occurred since President Bush took office in January 2001. Former Secretary of State Albright's visit to Pyongyang in October 2000 was indicative of a mutual willingness to engage. However, Pyongyang's continued willingness to engage has been stymied by President Bush's hard-line approach towards it, causing a strain in the relationship that is crippling future, short-term engagement opportunities. If the Agreed Framework is to succeed, the US must put aside any preconceived conditions for normalizing diplomatic and economic relations, and begin the normalization process now, an essential confidence-building measure. Though the Agreed Framework is designed to effect this normalization process, it has yet to accomplish it. Since the regime change that was anticipated has not occurred, the only viable alternative way to establish such a relationship is through engagement. With both sides apparently not willing to move forward quickly to achieve this goal, the acceptability of fully implementing the Agreed Framework is clearly in question.

Secondly, LWRs produce plutonium that can be used in making nuclear weapons; this issue is closely tied to the first issue. Because of the capability to misuse LWRs, the transfer of this technology must be based upon a relationship of trust--which is built over time--through political and economic engagements. Because the US has always been concerned about the misuse of spent LWR fuel, it included in the *KEDO-DPRK Reactor Supply Agreement* the requirement for North Korea to "relinquish any ownership rights over the LWR spent fuel and agree to the transfer of the spent fuel out of its territory as soon as technically possible after the fuel is discharged, through appropriate commercial contracts" (VIII(3)). The contract itself is insufficient to prevent North Korea from expelling IAEA inspectors and reprocessing spent LWR fuel to create nuclear weapons if it so desired. Hence, the US does not currently trust North Korea to possess nuclear reactors. Therefore, the US finds it unacceptable to progress further with building the LWRs until North Korea begins the process of achieving compliance with the IAEA full-scope safeguards agreement, even then it is unlikely that the US or KEDO would still be willing to build the LWRs.

Thirdly, LWRs cannot safely operate on North Korea's power grid. This issue was a concern that KEDO addressed in the *KEDO-DPRK Reactor Supply Agreement*. As a stipulation to transferring LWRs to North Korea, the supply agreement states: "the DPRK shall assure that appropriate nuclear regulatory standards and procedures are in place to ensure the safe operation and maintenance of the LWR plants . . . " [in accordance with a] "set of codes and standards equivalent to those of the IAEA and the US" (Articles X(3) and I(3)). However, since North Korea has not yet repaired its power grid so that it can achieve minimum LWR operating safety standards, the transfer of LWRs to North Korea is unacceptable. Likewise, it is financially unacceptable for KEDO to build the LWRs until a solution to this issue has been resolved.

Because of the regulatory stipulations that govern the transfer of key nuclear components to North Korea, the potential exists for discord to arise between the US and South Korea. As the LWR project is delayed, so is North Korea's responsibility to repay KEDO the cost of this project.[15] Since North Korea's power grid does not meet regulatory safety compliance, it is possible that this problem could eventually be the final issue that holds up completion of the LWR project. If the reactors are never brought on line, whatever money has been spent will be lost, and South Korea, saddled with 70 percent of the project cost, will lose the most. If perchance the US abandons the Agreed Framework it would likely lose some political capital, as well as financial capital. Lastly, KEPCO, South Korea's state owned energy company, sees this construction project as a step towards future contracts for building other reactors throughout the world. Therefore, the potential exists for South Korea to attempt to pressure the US into transferring the key nuclear components, regardless of North Korea's regulatory compliance, another issue that is potentially confrontational.

Suitability Test: Is the Full Implementation of the Agreed Framework a Suitable Means for Achieving the Denuclearization of the Korean Peninsula?

The Agreed Framework is in its eighth year, a remarkable feat considering that no other US policy instrument has accomplished this much progress with Pyongyang. Even so, the initial planning assumptions of the Agreed Framework were wrong. Primarily, the assumption that the

51

North Korean regime would be replaced by a more reasonable successor who would reform the government and improve the security environment of the Korean Peninsula has not yet occurred.

The Agreed Framework has been delayed by no fewer than six to seven years, or nearly twice its intended duration. Certainly, if US policymakers placed stock in their initial assumption that a political implosion of North Korea was likely during this period, delaying the project made some sense. However, since an implosion no longer appears likely, the real threat is that the Agreed Framework will breakdown and not achieve the denuclearization of North Korea, or that project delays will provide North Korea the time to covertly develop nuclear weapons, more than if there had been no agreement. If this greater nuclear weapons development turns out to be the case, then the current short-term gain of regional security would have been achieved at the expense of longer-term global security.

The Agreed Framework is an unsuitable policy option for denuclearizing North Korea. In fact, rather than creating an environment that reduces North Korea's ability to produce nuclear weapons, the LWRs, a plutonium generating system, if transferred, will significantly increase its capability to produce such weapons. Nuclear reactors and their technology should only be transferred to trustworthy, reliable partners. Since the US does not trust North Korea to operate its graphite-moderated reactors for fear that it will divert plutonium for use in building nuclear weapons, the transferring of LWRs is incomprehensible. The same controlling agency used to regulate the one would be used to regulate the other, the IAEA.

Given time and a committed effort by both parties, it is plausible, though unlikely in the near future, that the Agreed Framework could act as a conduit for building trust within US-North Korea relations. Confidence-building measures are the only way that any denuclearization agreement is going to achieve its end state. Some basic confidence-building measures that should be initiated include: (1) establishing regular communications between nations, such as opening capital-city liaison offices; (2) holding regular staff talks and conferences; (3) conducting regular senior diplomat and military officer counterpart visits; (4) normalizing economic trade relations; and (5) conducting meaningful humanitarian work inside North Korea. As these type of meaningful confidence-building measures take hold, mutual trust will begin to develop and the chasm of distrust that exists between the US and North Korea will begin to shrink. Until this occurs, it is unrealistic to expect that an action as complicated as denuclearizing North Korea could happen. Hence, the results of this analysis suggests that, given the current political direction of the US coupled with the aforementioned obstacles, the Agreed Framework is an unsuitable policy option for achieving the permanent or long-term denuclearization of North Korea.

The Amended Framework Option

On 16 February 2001, Doctors David Von Hippel and Peter Hayes of the Nautilus Institute's Energy, Security and Environment Program,[16] published a paper titled *Modernizing the US-DPRK Agreed Framework: The Energy Imperative.* Their paper, written from a position of twenty years experience analyzing Korean energy, security and policy issues, including experience working in North Korea, analyzes the Agreed Framework and provides a recommendation for amending the agreement. This Nautilus Institute proposal was used as the basic amended framework policy option. Additionally, an expanded analysis of several alternative solutions for ameliorating North Korea's present energy sector dilemma is provided.

Background Information on the Status of North Korea Energy

Heavy Fuel Oil Shipments

The Nautilus Institute recommends that in place of HFO deliveries, the US should offer to improve North Korea's power grid. Annually, the US, through KEDO, provides North Korea with 500,000 metric tons of HFO. In accordance with the Agreed Framework, the US is obligated to provide this HFO until completion of the first LWR. The first LWR, originally scheduled for completion in 2003, has been beset with multiple delays and is now projected for completion no earlier than 2009 (*Tokyo Shimbum* 29 December 2001).

The Department of State's foreign operations fiscal year 2002 budget request includes $95 million for KEDO. Of this amount, approximately $90 million is designated to fund the purchase and delivery of 500,000 tons of HFO shipments for 2002 (United States Department of State 2002, 272). Assuming that this cost remains stable until the first LWR is operational, the projected cost to the US over the next eight years would be $760 million. This may be an optimistic estimate because the record shows the cost has continued to increase,[17] from a low of $22 million in 1996 to a high of $95 million in 2002 (United States Department of State 2002, 272).

In accordance with the Agreed Framework, HFO delivered by KEDO is restricted to two uses--heating and electricity production. Certainly, the need for HFO is evident, but North Korea is incapable of consuming KEDO's annual shipment of 500,000 metric tons. North Korea has only one large oil-fired power plant and that is their 200-megawatt plant at Unggi, near the Russian border (Savada 1993, 149). Coal-fired power plants, as a method of enhancing fuel efficiency, also burn KEDO-supplied HFO. This technique helps to offset what is reportedly the declining quality of coal used in power plants. Consequently, there are eight power plants using HFO, the Unggi plant and seven other coal-fired plants. In 1996, according to the Nautilus Institute, North Korea's HFO stocks constituted approximate 1,060,000 tons (500,000 tons of which was provided by KEDO). Furthermore, HFO consumption was estimated at 27 percent by industry, 27 percent by the Unggi plant, and 31 percent by coal-fired power plants. The remaining 15 percent of the HFO, over 150,000 tons or nearly a third of the KEDO supplied oil, was placed in storage (Von Hippel and Hayes 1997, 9).[18]

Considering the cost to the US to deliver 500,000 tons of HFO, contrasted with North Korea's limited use of this product, the Nautilus Institute recommends that the US, in

54

coordination with North Korea, explore alternatives for providing infrastructure assistance in lieu

of partial or total HFO deliveries. The Nautilus Institute identified five priority areas where

assistance is both necessary and useful: (1) help rebuild the transmission and distribution system,

(2) help rehabilitate power plants and other coal-using infrastructure, (3) help rehabilitate coal

supply and coal transportation systems, (4) assist with the development of alternative sources of

small-scale energy and the implementation of energy efficiency measures, and (5) work to open

opportunities for independent power producers to work in North Korea. To appreciate the

Nautilus Institutes' recommendations, the following analysis outlines the condition of North

Korea's power grid and energy resources.

Analysis of North Korea's Power Grid

Although North Korea can boast having some 500 electricity generating facilities,

reportedly only sixty-two major power plants operate as part of the interconnected transmission

and distribution (TD) grid. The remaining plants are either small, isolated hydroelectric facilities

or dedicated industrial plants. These sixty-two power plants include forty-two hydroelectric plants

and twenty thermal plants. Twenty hydroelectric plants, and ten thermal plants provide 60 percent

of the power (Von Hippel et al. 2001, 13).

Constructed in 1958, the unified electrical grid includes the aforementioned sixty-two

power plants, fifty-eight substations, and eleven regional transmission and dispatching centers

(Von Hippel and Hayes 1997, 11). According to South Korea's Ministry of Unification, as of

1998, North Korea's power facility capacity was 7.39 gigawatts (*Joong Ang Ilbo* [Daily News]

[Seoul] 1 May 2000), about one-sixth of South Korea's. However, of this amount, 1.09 gigawatts

are from facilities designated for closure and 4.3 gigawatts are from facilities that are shut down

for repairs. Therefore, the actual stable generating capacity is little more than two gigawatts

(*Dong-a Ilbo* [Daily News] [Seoul] 29 September 2000). Furthermore, due to coal shortages,

rundown facilities and a lack of repair parts, only 26 percent of the power plants in North Korea can actually be operated, which further reduces the nation's electric generating capacity to only 1.7 gigawatts. Annually, a mere 18,600 gigawatt hours are produced (*Korea Herald* [Seoul] 18 December 2000),[19] which accounts for far less than its electricity demand of 36,000 gigawatt hours (*Seoul Korea Daily* 21 June 2000). Comparatively, this is only 7.7 percent or one-thirteenth of South Korea's capacity. Antiquated transmission and distribution networks cause a significant loss of power, reducing the consumable amount of electricity to slightly more than 11,000 gigawatt hours, 4.6 percent of South Korea's consumption.

Analysis of North Korea's Transmission and Distribution Network

North Korea uses three types of transmission lines, 220,000 kilovolts, 110,000 kilovolts and 66,000 kilovolts lines, and two types of distribution lines, 66,000 kilovolts and 3,300 kilovolts lines. The power grid in North Korea operates at sixty hertz. However, frequency control is poor, and the actual frequency on the system falls between forty-seven to fifty-two hertz (Von Hippel et al. 2001, 12). The electricity dispatching system is inefficient, minimally or not at all automated, and prone to failure. Estimates of TD losses vary from an official 16 percent up to estimates of 50 percent (Von Hippel and Hayes 1997, 11). Telephone and telex, without the aid of automation or computer systems, reportedly operate connections between the elements of the TD system, contributing to the daily blackouts and brownouts (Von Hippel et al. 2001, 12).[20] Inadequately maintained transmission lines and substations further degrade the TD system. There are inadequate or missing insulators on power poles, noninsulated power lines, weak wire tension, and improper wire gauge. Finally, in many areas transmission wires have been scavenged for barter goods (Roberson 2000).

Analysis of North Korea's Energy Resources

The principal energy sources for generating electrical power in North Korea are water and coal. North Korean terrain and climate provide significant hydraulic resources for hydroelectric generation. Today, approximately 4,500 megawatts of hydroelectric capacity are installed, and estimates of hydroelectric potential in North Korea range from 10,000 to 14,000 megawatts (Von Hippel and Hayes 1997, 6). North Korea anthracite and brown coal resources, though ample in quantity, vary in quality. Recoverable coal reserves are estimated at between 600 million (United States Department of Energy 2002) and 1.8 billion tons (Savada 1993, 127).

In addition to coal, North Korea uses two other major sources of thermal energy, oil, and biomass waste. North Korea has no operating oil wells. Whereas in the past North Korea imported crude oil from China, Russia and Iran, today it is imported exclusively via pipeline from China (Von Hippel et al. 2001, 10). Biomass products produced to fuel electricity generation include wastes from agriculture, industry, and urban areas. Given the harsh growing conditions in the areas where trees could be planted, growing trees specifically to fuel electricity generation would seem to be impractical and unlikely.

In addition to hydroelectric and thermal resources, wind, solar, and tidal power provide varying potential for electricity generation. Of these three alternate power sources, the potential of wind power has been recently tested. On 5 October 1998, a private project funded by the W. Alton Jones Foundation in Virginia, built and installed seven wind turbines in Unhari Village, about thirty miles north of Nampo City on North Korea's west coast. This 11.5-kilowatt wind plant, still used today, powers the village's medical clinic, kindergarten, and household humanitarian electricity needs for twenty homes at a total project cost of $400,000 (*Windpower Monthly* May 1999). This form of electricity is useful in rural and isolated areas that are not connected to the transmission grid system.

Analysis of North Korea's Energy Sector Problems

North Korea is plagued by multiple energy-sector problems, among which are the following: (1) There is a shortage of oil products, particularly motor fuels, caused by a lack of foreign currency to pay for imports of crude oil and refined products. (2) Coal shipments are perpetually delayed because of railroad line maintenance and faulty equipment that causes fuel shortages and electric supply problems.[21] (3) Antiquated coal mining equipment and flooded coal mines perpetuate substandard mining. (4) Damaged power generating plants and a dilapidated TD system retard the nation's neglected and decaying energy industry.

As a result of the 1995 and 1996 floods, as much as 85 percent of North Korea's hydroelectric generating capacity was rendered unusable. The heavy rains falling on deforested hills and mountains caused severe erosion and runoff that filled impoundments with silt, thereby reducing the holding capacity of dams and clogging spillways and channels. Damage occurred to gates, turbines, and other mechanical equipment (Von Hippel and Hayes 1997, 10). Of these problems, the silted reservoirs may be the most difficult to fix, as it requires heavy equipment, and considerable time to accomplish.

Poorly maintained power generation facilities and a lack of or mismanaged fiscal resources have left North Korea unable to afford essential spare parts. Hence, the generating capacity of electric power stations is inefficient and breakdowns are frequent. As an example, the Supung hydroelectric power plant, with a 700-megawatt generating capacity, can generate electricity that reaches only 30 to 40 percent of its basic power generating capacity because of its old facilities. Because North Korea was unable to fund the Supung power plant's renovation and repairs, China, a joint plant operator, financed the repairs and now consumes 90 percent of the plant's generated electricity, further exacerbating the energy shortage (*ROK Daily* [Seoul] 30 September 2000).

An Expanded Analysis of North Korea's Energy Sector and Alternative Solutions

The South Korean government studied three methods for providing electricity support to North Korea (*ROK Daily* [Seoul] 30 September 2000). The first method entailed providing electricity across the demilitarized zone. The second method suggested constructing a power plant in the North. The third method proposed providing fuel, such as coal and gas, to power North Korea's existing plants.

Connecting Power Facilities

As previously indicated, North Korea's power grid is designed to operate at sixty hertz. Of the surrounding countries, South Korea's electricity system also operates at sixty hertz, while the electric systems of China and Russia both operate at fifty hertz. In order for North Korea to connect to either China's or Russia's electric grid, it would be necessary to convert from fifty to sixty hertz at the intersection of power grids.

Chang Yong Sik, former President of KEPCO, stated, "In South Korea, we have a big surplus of power, especially at night. Except for about 100 hours a year in daytime during summer when power consumption peaks, we can send sufficient power to North Korea all year. If we repair the substation in Uijongbu we will be able to connect our transmission lines with those of North Korea." Chang claims that South Korea could supply 3,500 gigawatt hours annually, since the local power demand between 10 PM and 8 AM falls short of supply capacity (*Chosun Ilbo* [Seoul] 28 May 2000).

In the short term, the direct supply of electricity from the South would be very difficult. First, it would take more than a year to connect some thirty kilometers of severed transmission lines between the countries (*Korea Herald* [Seoul] 18 December 2000). Additionally, because the two countries' transmission lines are incompatible, a costly interface must be installed. One possibility is the use of a converter. By installing a converter near the DMZ, either the electric current in South Korea 345,000 kilovolt lines could be lowered to 220,000 kilovolts or the electric current in South Korea 154,000 kilovolt lines could be increased to 220,000 kilovolts to be compatible with North Korea lines. The initial cost of reconnecting transmission lines and converting the power is estimated to be approximately $700 million (Sokolski 2001, 3). However, a greater problem is the fact that the North Korean power grid is in need of repair. Therefore, in order to provide power to more than a few major cities, a reliable energy grid would need to be built. The cost of such a project is undermined; however, in 1995, Pyongyang asked for $1 billion to refurbish its power grid. Also the State Department has estimated such a project to be about $750 million (Plunk 2001, 22), whereas the Nautilus Institute estimates the cost to be between $3 and $5 billion (Von Hippel et al. 2001, 12). Another concern is the cost associated with providing direct power to the north. It costs South Korea about $636 million to produce 500,000 kilowatts of electricity (*Korea Herald* [Seoul] 18 December 2000).

Power Supply Infrastructure Reconstruction

There are broadly two ways of cooperation for repair and maintenance of North Korea's power supply infrastructure. One is to provide equipment and parts that North Korea wants, and the other is for South Korean companies to rehabilitate,[22] operate, and maintain specific power plants or TD facilities designated by North Korea. However, many political and economic barriers exist. Supplying power generating facilities and parts to North Korea cannot take place in the form of normal trade because of North Korea's foreign exchange shortage. Additionally, barter trade could be difficult because of the high price of the parts involved and the limited choices of goods to purchase from North Korea.

In June 2000, KEPCO and Hyundai Engineering and Construction Company considered building two thermal electric power plants near Pyongyang. Each plant would have a capacity of 100,000 to 200,000 kilowatts, with a combined cost of nearly $500 million. An alternative was to repair existing hydroelectric power plants, thereby increasing their power output (*ROK Daily News* [Seoul] 21 June 2000). Of these two options, the repair of existing hydroelectric power plants would prove more useful. Regardless of how many thermal electric plants were built, the associated coal industry problems would shortly nullify any perceived gains.

Coal Aid

According to Chong U-Chin, a researcher at Seoul's Energy and Economy Institute, fuel aid affords the greatest short-term potential for success. In October 2000, lawmakers from the ruling Millennium Democratic Party proposed that the government use South Korea's coal reserves to help Pyongyang solve its chronic energy shortage. South Korea has twelve million

tons of stockpiled coal,[23] the maintenance of which cost taxpayer dollars (*Korea Herald* [Seoul]

21 October 2000). In addition, the coal piles cause environmental problems, as rainwater seeps

into the piles and then flows into nearby streams. As the South increases its reliance on nuclear

energy, the national coal reserve continues to increase. Seven million tons can operate a thermal

electric power plant of two gigawatts for a year (Von Hippel et al. 2001, 19). This would be the

equivalent of fueling approximately twenty-five North Korean thermal power plants for one year.

If only one million tons of coal were provided annually to North Korea, yearly power generation

could be increased by 1,600 gigawatt hours, or 8.6 percent of North Korea's annual output (*Joong

Ang Ilbo* [Seoul] 16 October 2000). Furthermore, South Korean produced coal has a higher

thermal capacity and is of a higher grade than coal used in North Korea plants, thereby providing

a boost to North Korea's power generating efficiency.

Finally, the financial aspect of providing coal to North Korea should be an easy

government policy decision. The coal, already paid for, requires no additional expenditure, save

the cost of transportation. Initially coal could be provided as aid, and later perhaps the North

would barter mineral mining rights (iron, bronze, gold, etc.) for coal shipments. Admittedly, the

completion of the Seoul-Sinuiju Railway will reduce both the logistical challenges and

transportation expenses. Presently, the only means of transporting coal to the North is by ship.

This method of transportation is complicated by two factors, first, North Korea has no harbors

exclusively designated for unloading coal, and second, South Korea has only one coal handling

port, Mukho Port, which is not accessible to large freighters.

Coal Mining Heavy Equipment

North Korea's coal output has decreased by more than one-half in the past decade. The

fall in coal production is partly explained by flooding, though more importantly, the easily

extracted coal has mostly already been mined, thus requiring heavy mining equipment to conduct

61

deep tunnel mining. On the other hand, in South Korea the declining demand for coal has left much idle equipment in coal mines. This could be used in North Korea to help boost the country's coal production.

The Amended Framework Option Compared to the Agreed Framework

The proposed amendment to the Agreed Framework would focus on refurbishing North Korea's power grid. This KEDO-led project would first conduct a joint KEDO-DPRK assessment to determine the exact needs and how best to proceed. The project objective should be to refurbish the power grid to permit the long-term safe operations of the LWRs. Following the joint assessment; project funding will have to be decided. Project funding could be made available by reducing HFO deliveries and transferring money saved into the power grid project. If more funding was required, North Korea, using a system of barter trade, could provide natural resource mining rights to KEDO.[24] Then mining and shipping companies hired by KEDO would extract the resources and transport them to a company that would sell the resources on the international market. The profits earned in this endeavor would provide required funding for the power grid project. Because of the decrepit state of North Korea's power grid, it is expected that a refurbishment project would encompass many of the various options that were previously analyzed: repairing power generating plants and TD stations, providing coal for use in thermal electric power plants, and providing equipment to conduct deep mining operations in North Korea. Finally, if required, the power grids of South and North Korea could be connected.

The amended framework option offers three benefits over a status quo option. The first benefit is a plan to avoid the anticipated impasse that will occur if North Korea is not able to meet the US and IAEA safety regulations for the LWR. The second benefit is another opportunity for confidence building, to include the chance for KEDO work teams to operate throughout the country, thereby increasing contacts with the North Korean populace, a step towards improving relations. Finally, the third benefit is a proactive attempt at cooperatively providing humanitarian assistance that does more than just throw money at the problem. Physical improvements in the country's energy sector could facilitate resurgence in the nation's production capability, which could complement Pyongyang's efforts to attract international business investors. This type of change could begin the course direction Pyongyang needs to transition to a more open society.

Because of the estimated $750 million cost, the State Department has rejected considering an energy grid refurbishment project in North Korea (Plunk 2001, 22). However, this project would cost about the same as delivering HFO shipments for the next eight years. If a refurbishment of North Korea's electrical grid was substituted for HFO shipments, little or no extra money would be involved.

The Amended Framework Option Evaluated

Feasibility Test: Would Full Implementation of the Amended Agreed Framework Presented above be Feasible?

The total financial cost of this amended framework is comparable to that of the Agreed Framework. However, if the Agreed Framework were infeasible because North Korea failed to finance the repairs of its power grid, the amended framework would offer a cooperative solution to cover the cost of such a project. This makes the amended framework a feasible policy option.

The dilapidated condition of North Korea power grid is indicative of the amount of time and resources that will be required to refurbish it. The exact resources that are required to undertake a power grid refurbishment project are uncertain, though estimates indicate that it would cost between $750 million to $5 billion. It is expected that project funding would come from multiple sources.

Firstly, North Korea wants assistance in repairing its power grid, and has stated its willingness to fund such a project by offering mineral mining rights as a method of payment. This is a similar system of payment that has been adopted for repaying the cost of the LWR project. Specifically, the *KEDO-DPRK Supply Agreement* states, "The DPRK may pay KEDO in cash, cash equivalents, or through the transfer of goods" (Art II(3)).

Secondly, if future HFO funds were substituted for a work project, it is expected that a minimum of $760 million could be made available in this way. Though there is no record to indicate North Korea's willingness to exchange HFO deliveries to fund the refurbishment of its power grid, it is feasible from the US point of view.

Thirdly, if the US was willing it could allocate additional federal funds to assist in financing the refurbishment of North Korea's power grid. Because KEDO is predominately protecting the interests of the US, evident by the fact the Agreed Framework is a bilateral accord that is signed exclusively by it and North Korea, one could infer that the US should be willing to expend greater resources, than are currently being committed. Notwithstanding, it is probable that this policy option will not result in an increased cost to the US, a critical element to maintaining political and public support.

Lastly, if the US would take the lead, additional international funds could be mustered. As required, the US could work with multinational banks and other partner countries to provide a coordinated effort to finance a North Korea power grid refurbishment project. Following these suggestions, it is feasible to resource this policy option.

Acceptability Test: Would an Amended Framework be Acceptable to All Parties?

The utility of the amended framework over the Agreed Framework relates specifically to its ability to alleviate one of the three reasons why the Agreed Framework was unacceptable--the safety of operating LWRs on North Korea's decrepit power grid. The other two unacceptability issues, though not directly assuaged by the amended framework policy option, could be indirectly affected. Specifically, this policy option allows the US-KEDO to remain positively engaged with North Korea during a period in which future engagements could prove difficult, particularly if the Agreed Framework stalls. Even though the amended framework is an improved policy option over the Agreed Framework, it is unacceptable because (1) political and economic engagement is currently undesirable; and (2) LWRs produce fissile material that can be used to create nuclear weapons.

Since North Korea has refused to accept thermal power reactors in lieu of LWRs, such an amendment would be unacceptable to it (Gilinsky 2000). Hence, LWRs are at the crux of the problem. Consequently, the future acceptability of this policy option is predicated on the US being able to trust North Korea to possess LWRs, and until that occurs the amended framework will remain unacceptable to the US.

Suitability Test: Would the Amended Framework Lead to Denuclearization?

As discussed in the analysis of the Agreed Framework, three issues threaten to derail the successful completion of the Agreed Framework. First is the capability of the LWRs to produce weapons-grade and reactor-grade plutonium. This directly relates to the second issue, which is North Korea's noncompliance with the US Energy Act of 1954. Third is the dilapidated state of North Korea's power grid, a serious obstacle to operating the LWRs in accordance with US and IAEA safety standards.

Of these three issues, as with the Agreed Framework, the first two, which are linked, are contingent upon US confidence that North Korea will not use the LWRs with the intent of producing nuclear weapons. The process of building a relationship of trust takes time and should, therefore, begin soon. The third issue, North Korea's inability to operate the LWRs in accordance with US and international safety standards, can be resolved by adopting the recommendations presented in the amended framework. Though an amended framework can assist in this process, no agreement will resolve the issue of creating a relationship of trust until the US embraces that goal as a policy objective. Therefore, assuming a US resolve to begin the process of building a relationship of trust, the amended framework will facilitate that process.

The verifiable denuclearization of North Korea cannot occur until the IAEA completes its full-scope safeguards inspections and the GMRs are dismantled. In accordance with the Agreed

Framework, the completion of the IAEA inspections should coincide with the completion of the first LWR, while the GMRs are to be completely dismantled by the time the second LWR is built. The amended framework helps facilitate the transfer of LWRs by repairing North Korea's power grid, an obstacle to completing the LWR project. However, as long as the US suspects that North Korea might attempt to build nuclear weapons, the transfer of LWRs, which produce significant amounts of fissile material, will not enhance a denuclearization environment. Therefore, the amended framework, in of itself, will not achieve the denuclearization of North Korea.

The Comprehensive Framework Option

In July 1998, the 105th Congress connected future KEDO funding to a presidential requirement to conduct an inquiry into North Korea's compliance with the freezing of its nuclear weapons program (United States Congress 1998, 32). In November 1998, President Clinton responded to this directive by tasking Dr. William J. Perry, former Secretary of Defense, to conduct an extensive review of the US policy toward North Korea. This review was completed on 12 October 1999 and was titled the *Review of United States Policy toward North Korea: Findings and Recommendations*. Consequently, this review, coupled with the 1994 Agreed Framework, serves as Washington's current policy toward Pyongyang.

Whereas the Agreed Framework focuses on verifiably eliminating North Korea's nuclear weapons program, the government's "comprehensive framework," as termed and defined by former Secretary of Defense William J. Perry, also includes the elimination of North Korea's long-range missile program. Dr. Perry acknowledges that the Agreed Framework has succeeded in verifiably freezing North Korea's plutonium production capabilities at Yongbyon and Taechon. However, he qualifies that assertion by stating that the urgent focus of US policy towards North Korea must be "to end [all of] its nuclear weapons and long-range missile-related activities" (1999, 3). Dr. Perry's report will serve as the basis for analyzing a comprehensive framework or, in other words, a policy that connects to the Agreed Framework additional demands upon North Korea.

The US government's "comprehensive framework" is a two-path strategy. The first path entails US bilateral negotiations with North Korea aimed at achieving three goals. The first goal is the verifiable assurance that North Korea does not have a nuclear weapons program. The second goal is the complete and verifiable cessation of testing, production, and deployment of missiles exceeding the parameters of the Missile Technology Control Regime.[25] The third goal is the complete cessation of export sales of such missiles and the equipment and technology associated with them (Perry 1999, 7). As North Korea agrees to US demands and moves to eliminate its threats of nuclear weapons and long-range missiles, the US would reciprocate by normalizing diplomatic relations, reducing economic sanctions, and taking "other positive steps" that would provide opportunities for North Korea. The second path is the route to be taken if North Korea rejects negotiations to eliminate its nuclear and missile threat. If this occurs, Dr. Perry asserts that the US and its allies must be prepared to enact "firm measures" that will persuade North Korea to follow the first path.

Though the Perry policy review was initiated before North Korea launched a modified Taepodong-1 missile over Japan on 31 August 1998, that event was likely an influential factor in Dr. Perry's policy recommendation to eliminate North Korea's long-range missile capability. The Taepodong-1, a two-stage medium range ballistic missile (MRBM), was configured with a third-stage booster equipped with a space launch vehicle (SLV). Although the third-stage failed to ignite and consequently crashed with the SLV into the ocean, the US was immediately awakened to North Korea's long-range missile capability, a capability that augured an emerging potential threat upon the homeland of the US.

In a statement before the US Senate Armed Services Committee on 7 March 2000, General Thomas A. Schwartz, Commander of the US Forces Korea, stated that North Korea's ballistic missile inventory includes over 500 Scud missiles of various types and that it continues to produce and deploy Nodong, medium-range missiles. The gravity of General Schwartz's statement is readily apparent when considering that all of North Korea's ballistic missiles are capable of delivering nuclear weapons.

Assuming that North Korea possesses a nuclear device, which it implied during the second round of high-level talks (Sigal 1998, 63), it could deliver such weapons to all parts of South Korea with Scud missiles and all of Japan with Nodong missiles; it could reach Alaska and Hawaii with 2-stage, Taepodong-2 intercontinental ballistic missiles (ICBM), and anywhere in the US with its 3-stage, Taepodong-2 ICBM. Table 1 provides a summary of North Korea's ballistic missiles and their capabilities.

Table 1. North Korean Ballistic Missiles

Name/Type	Stages	Propellant	Range	Miscellaneous
Scud B/ Hwasong-5 SRBM	1	Liquid	300km	North Korea has over 500 Scud missiles of various types in its inventory.
Scud C/ Hwasong-6 SRBM	1	Liquid	600km	
Nodong MRBM	1	Liquid	1,300km	Large inventory of Nodong missiles in stock and exported.
Taepodong-1 MRBM	2	Liquid	2,000km	Tested 31 August 1998
Taepodng-1 SLV ICBM	3	Liquid /Solid	5,000km* estimated	Tested 31 August 1998 *Light Payload could hit the US
Taepodong-2 ICBM	2	Liquid	10,000km	Not yet tested
Taepodong-2 SLV ICBM	3	Liquid /Solid	15,000km	Not yet tested
SRBM - Short Range Ballistic Missile < 1,000 km MRBM - Medium Range Ballistic Missile 1,000-2,500 km ICBM - Intercontinental Range Ballistic Missile >2,500 km Sources: United States Department of Defense, *Proliferation Threat and Response*, 2001; Central Intelligence Agency, *CIA National Intelligence Estimates of Foreign Missile Development and the Ballistic Missile Threat through 2015*, 2002.				

The Comprehensive Framework Option Evaluated

The US government's "comprehensive framework" admittedly does not address certain issues that are critical to both Korea and Japan, such as the elimination of short-range and intermediate-range ballistic missiles, both of which are nuclear and biochemical capable. Regarding chemical and biological weapons, the review suggests that this issue would be better addressed multilaterally. Finally, this review does not address the North's large standing conventional military force.

The major difference between a comprehensive framework policy option and the Agreed Framework is the attempt to reduce North Korea's military offensive capabilities. Coupling the current US policy toward North Korea with its recent demands, a proposed comprehensive framework would include the following: (1) North Korea would eliminate all nuclear, biological, and chemical weapons stocks and production capabilities; and (2) it would reduce the overall size of its conventional military, with particular emphasis on its forward-deployed artillery and ground forces.

In exchange for these North Korean concessions, it is expected that the US would have to make several reciprocal agreements. First would be the normalization of diplomatic and economic relations. Second, because North Korea's economy relies heavily on the export of its weapons, with the halting of missile sales the allied side would probably have to develop an alternative source of revenue for North Korea. Though this would most likely initially occur in the form of aid, eventually, this could be exchanged for US, Japanese, and South Korean imports of North Korean exports. Additionally, because of the missile development prohibition, the US would have to agree to launch space satellites for North Korea. Finally, as North Korea withdraws conventional forces from near the DMZ, South Korea would have to reciprocate in kind.

Feasibility Test: Is Implementation of a Comprehensive Framework Feasible?

In addition to the current costs associated with the Agreed Framework, the major additional economic costs that would be incurred under this policy option are the costs of launching space satellites and providing financial aid in exchange for a North Korean moratorium on its missile production and sales. The cost of supplanting North Korea's annual export of ballistic missiles would be approximately $500 million (Reiss 1995, 233). It is expected that the US would seek allied cost sharing for this project; however, given KEDO's current financial constraints, it is unlikely that much of this additional cost could be distributed amongst allies, leaving the US with the bulk of all additional costs. Given the federal budget, the US could fund its portion of this policy option. However, like the Agreed Framework, this policy option requires North Korea to repair its power grid, making this policy option financially infeasible.

Acceptability Test: Would a Comprehensive Framework be Acceptable to All Parties?

Like the Agreed Framework, the comprehensive framework does not address the US aversion to engaging North Korea. Neither does it address the proliferation characteristics of the LWR. Nor does it address North Korea's inability to conform to the nuclear regulatory and safety standards of the US and the IAEA, a prerequisite for transferring the LWRs.

Also, the proposed comprehensive framework is so large that the probability of successfully implementing it is marginal. Because the Agreed Framework is far from being completed, it is unlikely that Pyongyang will consider signing another agreement with Washington. Additionally, the proposed US reciprocal measures normalizing diplomatic relations and eliminating economic sanctions were already conceded as reciprocal measures in the Agreed Framework. Nor is it likely that North Korea would acquiesce to a policy that attached conditions to the Agreed Framework. As an example, in 1999 the US announced that it had detected an underground nuclear weapons site in a remote mountainous area of northwestern North Korea called Kumchang-ri. The US, demanding immediate authorization to inspect the area, but eventually had to provide $200 million in food assistance for the privilege of inspecting an empty cave (National Intelligence Council 2001, 20).

The comprehensive framework is an expensive proposition; however, it is unlikely that the US could avoid the associated costs, if it expected North Korea to discontinue its missile program. Considering past congressional opposition to providing the monies that the US agreed upon under the Agreed Framework, a comprehensive framework that entails an increased financial responsibility to the US would be unacceptable.

Dr Perry emphatically stated that war should be avoided, but that "firm and measured steps" will be required if North Korea does not yield. Since the end of the Korean War, the US has brandished the "stick" at North Korea, and not once has it achieved a substantial result. Rather, the US, after too many confrontations with North Korea, has walked away after publicly eating a slice of humble pie. Therefore, this type of policy option is only likely to result in a loss of progress made and a reisolation of North Korea, making it unacceptable.

Suitability Test: Would a Comprehensive Framework Achieve Denuclearization?

In 1994, it was not that the Clinton administration was indifferent about Pyongyang's ballistic missile program, chemical weapons program, or its one million-man army poised along the DMZ. Rather, it understood the necessity of isolating the most critical security issue and pursuing it first. Any attempt at attaching additional conditions to the Agreed Framework is unlikely to yield success, and instead is more likely to challenge US integrity in regards to its ability to fulfill the only contract it has ever signed with Pyongyang--the Agreed Framework. Hence, the comprehensive framework is not an effective policy option for achieving the denuclearization of North Korea.

The Coercive Denuclearization Option

On 7 December 1993, Secretary of Defense Les Aspin, pursuant to Presidential Decision Directive 18 (PDD 18), announced a new defense policy for dealing with the possible spread of weapons of mass destruction. This policy was termed the *Defense Counterproliferation Initiative*. Counterproliferation Initiative (CPI),[26] a three-part strategy, includes actions that: (1) reduce the threat, (2) deter the threat, and (3) defend against the threat. Defining the policy, Les Aspin stated that, in addition to the traditional and principal methods of deterring proliferation of WMD,[27] CPI would also provide a capability for the US to deal with a "Saddam Hussein with nukes" (Schneider 1995, 2).

Though Aspin's remarks are rather ambiguous, in 1997, the Department of Defense, in its second issue of *Proliferation: Threat and Response*, clearly articulated its roles in conducting counterproliferation missions. The Department of Defense's counterproliferation response to WMD proliferation includes three forms: (1) preventing international proliferation, (2) protecting US citizens and allies, and (3) eliminating NBC targets using counterforce capabilities. According to the Department of Defense, counterforce operations, which include attacking NBC production facilities, storage complexes, and deployed mobile platforms, must be able to interdict an adversary's NBC capabilities at each step of an agent's employment (United States Department of Defense 1997, 71). Additionally, Barry Schneider of the National Defense University suggests that CPI includes reactive and preemptive measures. He says, in accordance with Article 51 of the UN Charter, preemptive strikes are limited to incidents involving self-defense, though many nations, including the US, understands this article includes incidents of anticipatory self-defense (Schneider 1995, 2).[28]

Historically, there have been eight incidents of preemptive counterproliferation strikes against nuclear weapons and nuclear weapon production sites.[29] Of these eight cases, a brief summary of three are provided in order to illustrate some applicable precedents between historical cases of PCP and a coercive denuclearization policy option.

Review of Historical Incidents of Preemptive Counterproliferation

<u>Iraq, Osiark-1 Nuclear Reactor</u>

In 1976, Iraq contracted with a French company to build a forty-megawatt nuclear reactor. During the five years that followed, the Israeli government, divided over the extent of this perceived threat, debated response options. Advocating restraint, the Israeli Labor Party advised diplomatic measures as the appropriate channel for resolving the issue. Menachem Begin, the Israeli Prime Minister and leader of the Likud Party rejected the notion as foolhardy. Begin, a survivor of both world wars, had fought desperately for the establishment of Israel and he was not about to allow an Arabic nation to arm itself with nuclear weapons. On 7 June 1981, during his final months in office, Begin ordered the Israeli Air Force to destroy the Osirak-1 nuclear reactor. The decision to conduct the PCP strike required serious contemplation of its possible consequences. Such an act can result in international condemnation, UN censorship, reprisal, or an escalation to war. Ariel Sharon, Israel's Prime Minister since February 2001, said in 1981, while serving as the Agriculture Minister, the Osirak-1 strike decision "was perhaps the most difficult decision which faced any [Israeli] government during all the years of the state's existence" (Weissman and Krosney 1981, 8).

The Israeli PCP strike upon Osirak brought immediate international condemnation and Iraq, through the UN, sought redress. As a result, Israel was chastised under UN Security Council Resolution 487. Ten years later, following the victory in the Gulf War, US Secretary of Defense Richard Cheney, during a speech before the Jewish Institute for National Security Affairs, reversed the US position of the Osirak attack by saying, "Let me tonight in front of this group thank my good friend David Ivry for the action Israel took in 1981 with respect to the [Osirak] reactor."[30] He added: "There were many times during the course of the build-up in the Gulf and the subsequent conflict that I gave thanks for the bold and dramatic action that had been taken [by Israel] some ten years before" (Cheney 1991).

73

The Osirak-1 PCP strike undisputedly derailed Iraq's weapons-grade plutonium capability. Consequently, the US, lulled into a false sense of security, inaccurately surmised that Iraq had ceased its nuclear weapons program. However, Iraq had actually transitioned from its large vulnerable plutonium-239 based nuclear weapons program to an indiscernible and clandestine uranium-235 based program (Watts and Keaney 1993, 314). In 1991, the IAEA, following the Gulf War, discovered that Iraq had successfully employed three techniques for producing uranium-235: EMIS using calutrons, chemical enrichment, and gaseous-centrifuge enrichment (Ekeus 1991, 4). Iraq not only pursued a secret program for developing enriched uranium, it contrived an elaborate international deceptive screen that successfully deceived both the UN and the US. The techniques Baghdad employed included misleading IAEA inspectors, constructing mock facilities, concealing and dispersing research materials and equipment, and employing middlemen and front companies to purchase sensitive items (Kay 1995, 85).

Iraq, Tuwaitha Nuclear Research Center and Mobile Scud Launchers

During the Gulf War, Iraq fired eighty-eight Scud missiles at Israel, Saudi Arabia, and Bahrain (United States Defense Intelligence Agency 1991, 1). Though many of these missiles were intercepted, out of 1,500 counterstrikes against Scud related targets there were no confirmed reports of destroying any of the mobile Scud missile launchers (United States Defense Intelligence Agency 1991, 1). According to the Gulf War Air Power Survey, a key lesson learned was how difficult it is to target mobile launchers.

During the war, limited intelligence about Iraq's nuclear program resulted in allied bombing of but two facilities--Tuwaitha Nuclear Research Center and the al-Saffa Uranium Enrichment Factory. Al-Tuwaitha, located thirty km south of Baghdad, was the location of Iraq's Tuwaitha Nuclear Research Center (NRC). The research center, established in 1960, contained all of Iraq's nuclear reactors--Osirak-1 (40-megawatt), Osiarak-2 (0.5-megawatt), and the five-megawatt Soviet-built research reactor. The bombing of Tuwaitha NRC destroyed what remained of Iraq's plutonium production facilities--Osirak-2 and the Soviet-built research reactor. The most significant aspect of the Tuwaitha bombing is the fact that this was the first time that an operating nuclear reactor was attacked, consequently, contaminating the area with radiation (Muller et al. 1994, 131).

Iraq, Zaafaraniyah--Uranium Enrichment Facilities

On 19 April 1991, UN Special Commission (UNSCOM)-Iraq was established to enforce UN Security Council Resolution 687, a post Gulf War disarmament mandate (United Nations Security Council 1991, SCR 687). In particular, Part C of the Resolution, required unconditional destruction of all Iraqi NBC weapons. On 17 January 1993, following Iraq's disruption of UNSCOM inspections, the US Navy conducted a Tomahawk Land Attack Missile (TLAM) strike against the Zaafaraniyah uranium enrichment facilities, destroying much of it.

Lessons Learned from Preemptive Counterproliferation

A brief examination of these historical vignettes of PCP attacks reveals three valuable lessons. The first is the utility of PCP strikes, which was sufficiently demonstrated in each instance it was employed. However, like the Osirak attack, the necessity of attack has often not been made evident for many years. For the US government, the endorsement of peacetime PCP occurred in 1993, when the US adopted counterproliferation as a new approach to nonproliferation of WMD. The second and third lessons to be learned are the fallibility of intelligence coupled with the inherent difficulties of targeting, which prevent PCP strikes from totally eliminating an enemy's nuclear weapons program and capabilities. Flawed US intelligence, as demonstrated during the Gulf War, prevented the allied forces from targeting a preponderance of Iraq's nuclear weapons production facilities, while flawed targeting prevented the allied forces from destroying nuclear capable, mobile Scud launchers. These lessons are particularly poignant when applied to an adversary like North Korea, which has powerful retaliatory options, specifically, the ability to destroy Seoul from hardened artillery positions along the demilitarized zone.

The Effects of Economic Sanctions in Coercive Denuclearization

When engaging in coercive denuclearization, a precursor of PCP might include economic sanctions. Considering China's veto of the 12 March 1993 Security Council Resolution (condemnation of North Korea for NPT notification withdrawal),[31] obtaining UNSC approval for sanctions against North Korea may well be a difficult process (Gaffney 1993, 2). Senator McCain, in his aforementioned report to Congress, offers two specific recommendations in regards to approaching the issue of sanctions. First, he suggested that prior to approaching the Security Council, the US must quietly but sternly notify both China and Russia that their failure to support or ratify sanctions will constitute an "insurmountable impasse in our relations" (United States Congress 1994, 8). Second, he stated that the Japanese government must block all remittances from Korean-Japanese to North Korea.

The ties between Korean-Japanese and North Korea can be traced back to 1955, when the General Association of Korean Residents, or *Chongryon,* was established. This organization, with its head office in Tokyo and branches in each prefecture, has a membership of 200,000, and serves as North Korea's de facto diplomatic representation in Japan. Among the organization's principal functions is the transferring of currency from Japan to North Korea. Most of this money has been generated through Korean ownership of many of Japan's 18,000 pachinko (pinball) parlors, which generate annual sales of $280 billion (*The Washington Post* 7 June 96). Though actual contributions are unknown, figures range between $600 million, as reported by Japanese police in 1994 (*The Washington Post* 7 June 1996), to $1.8 billion or 40 percent of North Korea's foreign exchange inflows, as stated by Senator McCain that same year (United States Congress 1994, 6). On 30 November 2001, during the US-led war on terrorism, Japan conducted its first

76

raid upon *Chongryon* in its first steps to curtail the transfer of funds to North Korea (*New York Times* 1 December 2001).

North Korea has stated that economic sanctions are paramount to a declaration of war (Oberdorfer 1997, 311). Whether or not imposing economic sanctions would actually prompt North Korea to military action, though, is uncertain. It is plausible, however, that it would lash out in some provocative form. Because of past North Korean threats to reinitiate their nuclear weapons program if economic sanctions are employed, it could be inferred that this would be the expected response. Also, given North Korea's history of terrorist activities against South Korea, it is plausible to expect that it would engage in terrorism against the US, Japan, and South Korea.

The Coercive Denuclearization Option Evaluated

Coercive denuclearization would likely follow a three-phase process: (1) a call for the imposition of UN approved economic sanctions, (2) a buildup of military forces on the peninsula and within the region, and (3) a preemptive TLAM strike by the US upon all known sites where WMD were manufactured and stored. However, because of the ubiquity of underground military facilities (approximately 10,000), within North Korea, many sites would be invulnerable to this form of attack.

To be most effective, economic sanctions must be approved by the UN and actively supported by the regional powers. As stated earlier, among the UN's five permanent Security Council members, China could be expected to veto resolutions imposing economic sanctions on North Korea. However, assuming that China could be convinced to either approve or abstain from voting on a motion to impose economic sanctions or military action against North Korea, there is no precedent to suggest that it would do this without North Korea first committing a provocative act. Assuming such an incident, it is likewise plausible to presuppose that the other regional players would also support economic sanctions. Though to be effective, sanctions would require the halting of China oil exports to North Korea, the end of Korean-Japanese fund transfers to

North Korea, and the cessation of all South Korean exports to the North. This would have to be augmented by naval blockades of the North's coast to prevent both imports and exports, with special emphasis on arms sales. Considering the great difficulty in stopping trade activity across the Chinese and Russian borders during the Korean War, it is skeptical as to how effectively these borders could be closed today. Also as inter-Korean trade continues to increase, there is a direct corollary with the decreasing popularity for the South Koreans to impose such sanctions, especially when considering the plans of various South Korean corporations to open manufacturing plants in North Korea.

Feasibility Test: Would Effective PCP Strikes against North Korea be Possible or Feasible?

Assuming that North Korea would not retaliate to a preemptive TLAM attack, an unrealistic assumption, it would cost the US, $1.4 million for each TLAM it used. As an example, the US in its 1993 TLAM attack upon Iraq fired forty-four TLAMs, which applying today's cost would be $61.6 million. Though such a sum is economically feasible, the caves of North Korea make it virtually impossible to detect or destroy all possible targets. Hence, the coercive denuclearization policy option, though it could destroy all of North Korea's known nuclear weapons production site, would be incapable of destroying any unknown covert sites.

Moreover, such an attack could initiate a conventional North Korean artillery barrage on Seoul, and bring about the undesirable consequences and expenses required to fighting a second Korean War. Notwithstanding, some, to include House Defense Appropriations Subcommittee Chairman John Murtha (Democrat-Pennsylvania), think that the US should not only follow a path of coercive denuclearization; it must also follow up by being postured to prosecute a war (Gaffney 1993, 3). It has been reported that Operation Plan 5027, the Korean Peninsula war plan, requires 400,000 reinforcements in order to execute combat operations in Korea (Oberdorfer 1997, 325).

In a comparison of military campaigns, during Operation Desert Storm the US deployed 469,000 troops and spent $61 billion (United States Department of Defense 1992, Appendix P). However, because the US active military is much smaller than it was during the Gulf War, its current ability to fight a major theater war is now, more than in 1991, predicated upon the necessity to mobilize both the National Guard and the Reserve Forces. These mobilized forces would be used to either fight in the Korean Theater, to stand ready as a credible deterrence against US enemies in other regions, or to conduct other current worldwide military operations. However, as costly as it would be for the US to fight a second Korean War, which feasibly it could be difficult to resource, a much greater cost would be the destruction of South Korea's infrastructure and the infliction of very heavy South Korean casualties, a cost that it finds infeasible.

Acceptability Test: Would Preemptive Counterproliferation be Acceptable?

South Korea would never accept a preemptive counterproliferation strike. During the escalation of military provocation on the Korean Peninsula by the US in 1994, the South Korean government was more concerned about overheated rhetoric and brinkmanship in Washington than about a North Korean nuclear threat. Consequently, President Kim Young Sam declared privately that he refused to be remembered in history as a culpable party to reinitiating a second Korean War (Oberdorfer 1997, 302). Nor is it likely that any future South Korean government would support such a policy option.

Since the inauguration of President Kim Dae Jung in 1998, Seoul has embraced North Korea in a peaceful engagement policy that is often referred to as the "Sunshine Policy." Certainly, a policy of coerciveness would be in direct confrontation with South Korea's engagement policy.

Not only would this policy option derail security in Northeast Asia, it would most certainly worsen relations with China, and would potentially damage relations with South Korea and Japan, potentially affecting US influence within the region. Nor would other US Allies accept this policy option, except maybe under extreme circumstances. Lastly, it is inconceivable to imagine initiating any conflict that would cause as much death and destruction upon US servicemen or its allies as this policy option is likely to produce; consequently, it is unacceptable.

Suitability Test: Would Preemptive Counterproliferation Achieve Denuclearization?

Coercive denuclearization would employ the "stick" as a sole means of forcing North Korea to conform to denuclearization. Certainly from the viewpoint of many right-wing conservatives, a good characteristic of this policy option is the employment of preeminent power to force an adversary to capitulate to the will of both the US and the UN. Theoretically, this policy option is designed to inflict enough pain upon North Korea to change its behavior. However, ten years of UN enforced economic sanctions against Iraq have shown that a determined antagonist can endure. Neither have US imposed trade restrictions against North Korea, coupled with natural disasters of drought and flooding, which have been prevalent in North Korea over the past decade, brought about the anticipated implosion of the communist regime.

Like the 1993 US TLAM attack against Iraq's Zaafaraniyah uranium enrichment facilities, the US has the capability of conducting PCP attacks upon all suspected North Korean nuclear weapons production sites. However, like the Israeli attack on Iraq's Osirak-1 nuclear power plant, the destruction or elimination of overt nuclear weapons production facilities at Yongbyon and Taechon will not prevent North Korea from pursuing a covert nuclear weapons program.

A preemptive attack would almost assuredly invoke a retaliatory attack by North Korea upon South Korea. Whether the North would respond by conducting an artillery attack upon Seoul or by choosing another form of retaliation, such as attacking a South Korean nuclear power plant, either scenario would be devastating. Likewise, rather than creating an environment that

80

would encourage North Korea to abandon its nuclear weapons program, a PCP policy might galvanize its will to complete such a project. Among the four policy options, coercive denuclearization is a policy option that is least likely to enhance the security of allies, and is most likely to abrogate the US continued legitimate and consensual influence within the region. Therefore, this policy option is considered unsuitable.

The *National Security Strategy* of the US declares the denuclearization of North Korea to be of vital national interest, and hence, for the past eight years the US has attempted to achieve that objective by way of the Agreed Framework. Critics of the Agreed Framework have offered alternative suggestions, three of which were evaluated in this study, as to how best to achieve the denuclearization of North Korea. This chapter has revealed the strengths and weaknesses of each of the four evaluated policy option, and in the final chapter a summation of these analyses is provided, along with some recommendations as to how the US might proceed in achieving its goal of denuclearizing North Korea.

---

[1] Ambassador Hubbard is the Ambassador to South Korea. Formerly, he served as the Principal Deputy Assistant Secretary of State for East Asian and Pacific Affairs from 7 August 2000 to 10 July 2001. As the Deputy Assistant Secretary of State for East Asian and Pacific Affairs from March 1993 to August 1996, he played a principal role in developing the Agreed Framework.

[2] In April 1965, the North Korean Central Committee announced its proposal for a three-tiered revolution. Revolution 1 called for the revolutionizing of North Korea's military might. Revolution 2 called for the erosion of South Korea's foreign military alliances, particularly targeting the removal of US Forces and nuclear weapons from South Korea. Revolution 3, the diplomacy turning strategy, was intended to align North Korea with various foreign countries while internationally isolating South Korea.

[3] It took the IAEA over three years to complete inspections of South Africa's nuclear program, a country that was cooperative with the Agency (Sokolski 2001, 2).

[4] A significant portion of the LWR project, referenced in Article III(c) of the Reactor Supply Agreement is defined in Annex 4 of the same. Holistically speaking the definition of the term requires completed construction of the turbine building, and reactor building and containment structure to the point suitable for the introduction of components of the nuclear steam supply system.

[5]This concern is a little suspect. If the first LWR will not be completed until 2009, logically inspections could be initiated in 2006 and still be completed by the time the LWR is completed.

[6]See KEDO-DPRK Reactor Supply Agreement, Articles I(3) and X(3-4).

[7]Currently, the DPRK's total generating capacity is only 1.7 GW (Dong-a Daily News [Seoul] 29 September 2000), less than the total amount of power that both LWRs combined will provide to the power grid (1 LWR is 1,000 MW = 1GW).

[8]When a reactor must be taken off-line quickly (as when the electrical frequency varies too greatly from design parameters), control rods must be inserted into the reactor core to "quench" the nuclear chain reaction. If a combination of several of these control rods are not inserted properly, and the more frequently reactors must be shut down, the more probable this event becomes, then the chain reaction could continue, with the possible results being an overheating of the reactor core.

[9]One bomb's worth of reactor-grade plutonium is 7 to 10 kg (Holdren 1989, 174).

[10]"In practice, at all burn-up levels and at any time following discharge the critical mass of reactor-grade plutonium metal is intermediate between that of Pu-239 and Pu-240, which is more reactive than weapons-grade uranium, reactor-grade plutonium can be brought to a supercritical--and hence, explosive-state by any assembly system that can handle U-235." (Mark 1993, 115).

[11]The Nagasaki bomb was 22 kilotons and was exploded at a height of burst of 1,640-feet. The Hiroshima bomb was 12.5 kilotons and was dropped at a height of burst of 1,670-feet.

[12]"[If] the president determines that cessation of such exports would be seriously prejudicial to the achievement of the United States nonproliferation objectives or otherwise jeopardize the common defense and security: Provided, that prior to the effective date of any such determination, the President's determination, together with a report containing the reasons for his determination, shall be submitted to the Congress and referred to the Committee on Foreign Affaires of the House of Representatives and the Committee on Foreign Relations of the Senate for a period of sixty days of continuous session, but any such determination shall not become effective if during such sixty-day period the Congress adopts a concurrent resolution stating in substance that it does not favor the determination." (1954 Atomic Energy Act, Chapter 11 Section 129).

[13]The South Korean portion of the project is complete and the North Korean portion has not yet started.

[14]Nations establishing diplomatic relations were Italy (January 2000), Australia (May 2000), UK (December 2000), Netherlands and Turkey (15 January 01), Belgium (23 January 2001), Canada (6 February 2001), Spain (7 February 2001), Germany (1 March 2001), Luxembourg (5 March 2001), Greece (8 March 2001), Brazil (9 March 2001), New Zealand (26 March 2001), Kuwait (6 April 2001), EU (14 May 2001), Bahrain (23 May 2001). Source www.korea-np.co.jp/pk/173rd_issue/2001122609.htm

[15]Once the reactors are completed and handed over to North Korea the DPRK will repay KEDO the cost of the project, interest free, over a 20-year term (see Appendix 4, Article II).

[16]Nautilus Institute is a nonprofit organization based in Berkeley, CA. The Institute's mission is to solve interrelated critical global problems by improving the processes and outcomes of global governance. The Nautilus Institute's Energy, Security & Environment Program, started in 1996, analyzes the nexus of energy, security, and environmental issues in NORTHEAST ASIA. Based on this analysis policy initiatives are developed. The twin fields of "environmental security" and "energy security," as applied in Northeast Asia, underlie much of the work of the program.

[17]Total United States KEDO expenditures from 1995 through 2002 are $331 million (M), an annual breakout follows: 1995--$4M, 1996--$22M, $1997--$25M, $1998--$40M ($25.7M of which was spent for capping fuel cells), 1999--$35M, 2000--$55M, 2001--$55M, 2002--$95M. These statistics are taken from the Department of States Congressional Budget Foreign Operations (1995 through 2002).

[18]No data is available for whether or not HFO was used for heating purposes.

[19]18,600 GWh per year allows each family to light only one incandescent lamp.

[20]An incident of low voltage.

[21]In the DPRK, 90% of the total cargo shipment and 60% of all passenger transportation is conducted by rail. Additionally, of the nation's 5,214 kilometers of rail line 79% is electrified (Chungan Chosun [Seoul] 17 August 2000).

[22] Reportedly, the ROK government contacted engineers from former East Germany who had technologically supported the DPRK's power facilities in the past.

[23]Currently, it cost about 90 dollars to purchase a ton of coal in the ROK.

[24]In December 2000, the author met with an Australian diplomat who had just returned from Pyongyang, where he led a group of experts on a mission to assess the DPRK's power grid. As they had expected, much work would be required before the grid could be fixed. The group was offered a contract to do some work, but they were impeded by the method of payment offered, natural resource mining rights.

[25]The regime controls are applicable to such rocket and unmanned air vehicles as ballistic missiles, space launch vehicles, sounding rockets, unmanned air vehicles, cruise missiles, drones and remotely piloted vehicles capable of delivering a 500 kilogram (1102 lb.) payload at least 300 kilometers (186 miles).

[26]CPI has five elements (1) creation of the new mission, (2) tailoring new US weapons to destroy WMD, (3) planning to fight wars differently, (4) focusing intelligence efforts on detecting WMD, (5) ensuring international cooperation in curtailing the treat of WMD.

[27]Traditional methods of deterring the proliferation of WMD include: diplomacy, treaty restrictions, security assurance, export controls, non-military sanctions and economic cooperation.

[28]Examples of the United States following the view of anticipatory self-defense would include the Cuban blockade in 1962, the 1986 raid on Libya, and the 1993 attack on Iraq's Zaafaraniyah industrial complex.

[29](1) During WW II, allied air attacks and acts of sabotage upon Nazi atomic laboratories successfully halted the German effort to build an atomic bomb. (2) 13 April 1945, the United States bombing of Tokyo destroyed a Japanese atomic bomb research laboratory. (3) 30 September 1980, during the Iran-Iraq War, Iranian aircraft attacked, but did not destroy, the Iraqi Osirak-1 Nuclear Reactor. (4) 7 June 1981, Israel conducted the world's first, peacetime preemptive air strike on Iraq's Osirak-1 Nuclear Reactor, destroying it. (5) In 1982, Israel planned a peacetime preemptive air strike against Pakistan's nuclear reactor in Kahuta. India refused Israeli's request to land and refuel Israeli bombers, thereby thwarting the intended mission. (6) Between 1984 to 1988, during the Iran-Iraq War, Iraq launched seven different air attacks against Iran's nuclear reactor in Bushehr, ultimately destroying it. (7) During the Gulf War, the United States conducted 1,500 strikes against nuclear capable Scud missiles and attacked Iraq's nuclear reactor at Al-Tuwaitha; the first time that an operational nuclear reactor was attacked (Muller 1994, 131). (8) On 17 January 1993, while enforcing United Nations Security Resolution 687, the United States launched 44 Tomahawk cruise missiles at Iraq's Zaafaraniyah industrial complex, a uranium enrichment production facility.

[30]David Ivry, the current Israel Ambassador to the US, is the former commander of the Israeli Air Force at the time of the Osirak attack.

[31]On 11 May 1993 the UNSC did pass SCR 825 condemning the DPRK's notification of withdrawal from the NPT (UNSC 1993, SCR825).

CHAPTER 5

CONCLUSIONS AND RECOMMENDATIONS

The denuclearization of North Korea, a formalized policy objective of the US since the signing of the 1994 Agreed Framework, remains the singularly most important objective of Washington regarding Pyongyang. However, because of inaccurate planning assumptions in developing the 1994 Agreed Framework, namely that Pyongyang was facing an imminent implosion, the advisability of providing LWRs to North Korea has come into question. In 1999, Washington, in reaction to a North Korea ballistic missile test, unilaterally attached to a provision in the Agreed Framework the demand for North Korea to eliminate its long-range ballistic missile programs. Then, in 2001, Washington, vexed by perpetual delays in the Agreed Framework, requested a meeting with Pyongyang to discuss a host of security concerns that included the proliferation of nuclear, biological and chemical weapons, long-range missiles, and the reduction of its military force. That meeting has yet to occur, and President Bush's characterization of North Korea as a member of an "Axis of Evil" in January 2002 has done little to advance the cause of engagement or NPT objectives in North Korea.

The security problems caused by Pyongyang will certainly not just go away. Therefore, if the US is to achieve the permanent or long-term denuclearization of North Korea, it needs to follow an effective policy. How this policy might be achieved has been examined from the viewpoint of four possible policy options: (1) continuing with the Agreed Framework, (2) amending the Agreed Framework, (3) adopting a more comprehensive framework, and (4) undertaking coercive denuclearization. Provided in the paragraphs that follow is a holistic view of these policy options.

While the first three policy options evaluated--the Agreed Framework, the amended framework, and the comprehensive framework--seek to resolve North Korea's nuclear weapons threat through negotiations, the fourth policy option, coercive denuclearization, seeks to exact

North Korea's compliance through economic sanctions and preemptive military attacks. Regardless of the method used, none of the evaluated policy options are calculated to achieve the long-term denuclearization of North Korea.

The first three policy options, hereafter referred to collectively as "negotiated frameworks," each used the 1994 Agreed Framework as its base-negotiating instrument, an accord that the author considers flawed. There are three main problems with the Agreed Framework. The first problem is that the transfer of LWRs to North Korea is supposed to reduce its ability to produce nuclear weapons, but in actuality the converse is true. North Korea relinquishes its GMRs, with a capability to produce enough fissile material to build thirty nuclear bombs annually (Sigal 1998, 91), for two LWRs that collectively produce enough fissile material to produce sixty to one hundred nuclear bombs annually--a 50 to 70 percent increase in capability. The trust required for North Korea to operate its GMRs without diverting plutonium to build nuclear warheads is the same trust that is required to operate LWRs. Since the US does not trust North Korea to operate its GMRs, it does not and should not trust North Korea to operate LWRs.

This matter of trust is the second problem with the Agreed Framework; in fact, it is the central problem of any agreement with North Korea. Since the Bush administration assumed office in Washington, the aversion that the US has with engaging North Korea has become more pronounced. The negotiated frameworks each rely upon a relationship of mutual trust to be successful, but current trends indicate that there is little desire to pursue such efforts. Until relationships of trust are forged between the US and North Korea, no LWR transfer agreement will succeed.

Thirdly, so long as the LWRs are unable to safely operate on North Korea's power grid, it is unsafe, and consequently prohibited by law, to transfer LWRs to North Korea. The success of the negotiated frameworks is predicated on the transfer of the LWRs to North Korea. Of the three framework agreements, the amended framework is the only agreement that proposes a solution to resolve the impasse in transferring LWRs that is created by North Korea's decrepit power grid. Notwithstanding this accomplishment, the amended framework, like the other two, is unsuitable for achieving the denuclearization of North Korea.

Though the negotiated frameworks fail to achieve the denuclearization of North Korea, they do not directly violate the other two US security objectives in Northeast Asia--enhancing the security of allies and maintaining influence in the region. The fourth policy option, coercive denuclearization, however, violates all three US security objectives in the region.

Unlike the negotiated frameworks, coercive denuclearization attempts to punish North Korea until it acquiesces to a policy of denuclearization. This policy option is dangerous and should be avoided in all circumstances. The probable failures from executing this policy option are numerous. Firstly, it is unlikely that PCP strikes alone could totally eliminate North Korea's nuclear weapons production capabilities, and even if it could, it would probably only be a temporary occurrence. A North Korean counterstrike upon South Korea or Japan could produce millions of dollars in damage, cause tens of thousands of casualties, and lead to the loss of US influence in the region.

This study, unfortunately, has not revealed a policy option that will lead to the denuclearization of North Korea. The principal fault of each evaluated policy option is the unrealistic expectation that enemies (the US and North Korea) could take one large step from a policy of exclusion to a policy of denuclearizing a nation. What is lacking is a desire to commit to a series of confidence-building measures, or small reciprocal steps designed to build trust to bridge the chasm of hate and distrust. However, the need for an effective policy option requires that the search continue; therefore, it is hoped that the work conducted in this thesis will be of some assistance for developing a policy option that will lead to the denuclearization of North Korea.

APPENDIX A

JOINT DECLARATION OF THE DENUCLEARIZATION
OF THE KOREAN PENINSULA

20 January 1992

To enter into force as of 19 February 1992

The South and the North, desiring to eliminate the danger of nuclear war through denuclearization of the Korean Peninsula, and thus create an environment and conditions favorable for peace and peaceful unification of our country and contribute to peace and security in Asia and the world, declare as follows:

1. The South and the North shall not test, manufacture, produce, receive, possess, store, deploy or use nuclear weapons.

2. The South and the North shall use nuclear energy solely for peaceful purposes.

3. The South and the North shall not possess nuclear reprocessing and uranium enrichment facilities.

4. The South and the North, in order to verify the denuclearization of the Korean Peninsula, shall conduct inspection of the objects selected by the other side and agreed upon between the two sides, in accordance with procedures and methods to be determined by the South-North Joint Nuclear Control Commission.

5. The South and the North, in order to implement this joint declaration, shall establish and operate a South-North Joint Nuclear Control Commission within one (1) month of the effectuation of this joint declaration.

6. This Joint Declaration shall enter into force as of the day the South and North exchange notifications of completion of the procedures for the entry into force of this declaration.

Signed on 20 January 1992

Chung Won Shik

Prime Minister of the
Republic of Korea

Chief Delegate of the South
for the South-North High-Level Talks

Yon Hyong Muk

Premier of the Administration Council of the
Democratic Peoples Republic of Korea

Chief Delegate of the North
for the North-South High-Level Talks

APPENDIX B

JOINT STATEMENT OF THE DEMOCRATIC PEOPLE'S REPUBLIC OF KOREA AND THE UNITED STATES OF AMERICA

New York, 11 June 1993

The Democratic People's Republic of Korea and the United States of America held government-level talks in New York from the 2nd through the 11th of June 1993. . . . At the talks, both sides discussed policy matters with a view to a fundamental solution of the nuclear issue on the Korean Peninsula. Both sides expressed support for the North-South Joint Declaration of the Denuclearization of the Korean Peninsula in the interest of nuclear nonproliferation goals.

The DPRK and the US have agreed to principles of:

- Assurance against threat and use of force, including nuclear weapons;
- Peace and security in a nuclear-free Korean Peninsula, including impartial application of full-scope safeguards, mutual respect for each other's sovereignty, and noninterference in each other's internal affairs; and
- Support for the peaceful reunification of Korea.

In this context, the two Governments have agreed to continue dialogue on an equal and unprejudiced basis. In this respect, the Government of the DPRK has decided unilaterally to suspend as long as it considers necessary the effectuation of its withdrawal from the Treaty on the Nonproliferation of Nuclear Weapons.

APPENDIX C

AGREED STATEMENT BETWEEN THE UNITED STATES OF AMERICA AND THE DEMOCRATIC PEOPLE'S REPUBLIC OF KOREA

Geneva, 12 August 1994

The delegations of the US and the DPRK met in Geneva from 5-12 August 1994, to assume the third round of talks.

Both sides affirmed the principles of the 11 June 1993, US-DPRK joint statement and reached agreement that the following elements should be part of a final resolution of the nuclear issue:

(1) The DPRK is prepared to replace its graphite-moderated reactors (GMR) and related facilities with light-water reactor (LWR) power plants, and the US is prepared to make arrangements for the provision of LWRs of approximately 2,000 megawatts to the DPRK as early as possible and to make arrangements for interim energy alternatives to the DPRK's GMRs. Upon receipt of US assurances for the provision of LWRs and for arrangements for interim energy alternatives, the DPRK will freeze construction of the 50-megawatt and 200-megawatt reactors, forego reprocessing, and seal the Radiochemical Laboratory, to be monitored by the IAEA.

(2) The US and the DPRK are prepared to establish diplomatic representation in each other's capitals and to reduce barriers to trade and investment, as a move toward full normalization of political and economic relations.

(3) To help achieve peace and security on a nuclear-free Korean Peninsula, the US is prepared to provide the DPRK with assurances against the threat or use of nuclear weapons by the US, and the DPRK remains prepared to implement the North-South Joint Declaration on the denuclearization of the Korean Peninsula.

(4) The DPRK is prepared to remain a party to the Treaty on the Nonproliferation of Nuclear Weapons and to allow implementation of its safeguards agreement under the Treaty.

Important issues raised during the talks remain to be resolved. Both sides agree that expert-level discussions are necessary to advance the replacement of the DPRK's GMR program with LWR technology, the safe storage and disposition of the spent fuel, provision of alternative energy, and the establishment of liaison offices. Accordingly, expert-level talks will be held in the US and DPRK or elsewhere as agreed. The DPRK and US agreed to recess their talks and resume in Geneva on 23 September 1994.

In the meantime, the US will pursue arrangements necessary to provide assurance for the LWR project to the DPRK as part of a final resolution of the nuclear issue, and the DPRK will maintain the continuity of safeguards, as agreed in the 20-22 June 1994, exchange of messages between Assistant Secretary of State Robert L. Gallucci and First Vice Minister of Foreign Affairs Kang Sok Ju.

APPENDIX D

AGREED FRAMEWORK BETWEEN THE UNITED STATES OF AMERICA AND THE DEMOCRATIC PEOPLE'S REPUBLIC OF KOREA

Geneva, 21 October 1994

Delegations of the governments of the United States of America (US) and the Democratic People's Republic of Korea (DPRK) held talks in Geneva from September 23 to October 21, 1994, to negotiate an overall resolution of the nuclear issue on the Korean Peninsula.

Both sides reaffirmed the importance of attaining the objectives contained in the August 12, 1994 Agreed Statement between the US and the DPRK and upholding the principles of the June 11, 1993 Joint Statement of the US and the DPRK to achieve peace and security on a nuclear-free Korean Peninsula. The US and the DPRK decided to take the following actions for the resolution of the nuclear issue:

I. Both sides will cooperate to replace the DPRK's graphite-moderated reactors and related facilities with light-water reactor (LWR) power plants.

1. In accordance with the October 20, 1994 letter of assurance from the US President, the US will undertake to make arrangements for the provision to the DPRK of a LWR project with a total generating capacity of approximately 2,000 megawatts by a target date of 2003.
   - The US will organize under its leadership an international consortium to finance and supply the LWR project to be provided to the DPRK. The US, representing the international consortium, will serve as the principal point of contact with the DPRK for the LWR project.
   - The US, representing the consortium, will make best efforts to secure the conclusion of a supply contract with the DPRK within six months of the date of this Document for the provision of the LWR project. Contract talks will begin as soon as possible after the date of this Document.
   - As necessary, the US and the DPRK will conclude a bilateral agreement for cooperation in the field of peaceful uses of nuclear energy.

2. In accordance with the October 20, 1994 letter of assurance from the US President, the US, representing the consortium, will make arrangements to offset the energy foregone due to the freeze of the DPRK's graphite-moderated reactors and related facilities, pending completion of the first LWR unit.
   - Alternative energy will be provided in the form of heavy oil for heating and electricity production.
   - Deliveries of heavy oil will begin within three months of the date of this Document and will reach a rate of 500,000 tons annually, in accordance with an agreed schedule of deliveries.

3. Upon receipt of US assurances for the provision of LWR's and for arrangements for interim energy alternatives, the DPRK will freeze its graphite-moderated reactors and related facilities and will eventually dismantle these reactors and related facilities.
   - The freeze on the DPRK's graphite-moderated reactors and related facilities will be fully implemented within one month of the date of this Document. During this one-month period, and throughout the freeze, the International Atomic Energy Agency (IAEA) will be

allowed to monitor this freeze, and the DPRK will provide full cooperation to the IAEA for this purpose.
  - Dismantlement of the DPRK's graphite-moderated reactors and related facilities will be completed when the LWR project is completed.
  - The US and the DPRK will cooperate in finding a method to store safely the spent fuel from the 5-megawatt experimental reactor during the construction of the LWR project, and to dispose of the fuel in a safe manner that does not involve reprocessing in the DPRK.

4. As soon as possible after the date of this document US and DPRK experts will hold two sets of expert talks.
  - At one set of talks, experts will discuss issues related to alternative energy and the replacement of the graphite-moderated reactor program with the LWR project.
  - At the other set of talks, experts will discuss specific arrangements for spent fuel storage and ultimate disposition.

II. The two sides will move toward full normalization of political and economic relations.

1. Within three months of the date of this Document, both sides will reduce barriers to trade and investment, including restrictions on telecommunications services and financial transactions.

2. Each side will open a liaison office in the other's capital following resolution of consular and other technical issues through expert level discussions.

3. As progress is made on issues of concern to each side, the US and the DPRK will upgrade bilateral relations to the Ambassadorial level.

III. Both sides will work together for peace and security on a nuclear-free Korean Peninsula.

1. The US will provide formal assurances to the DPRK, against the threat or use of nuclear weapons by the US

2. The DPRK will consistently take steps to implement the North-South Joint Declaration on the De-nuclearization of the Korean Peninsula.

3. The DPRK will engage in North-South dialogue, as this Agreed Framework will help create an atmosphere that promotes such dialogue.

IV. Both sides will work together to strengthen the international nuclear nonproliferation regime.

1. The DPRK will remain a party to the Treaty on the Non-Proliferation of Nuclear Weapons (NPT) and will allow implementation of its safeguards agreement under the Treaty.

2. Upon conclusion of the supply contract for the provision of the LWR project, ad hoc and routine inspections will resume under the DPRK's safeguards agreement with the IAEA with respect to the facilities not subject to the freeze. Pending conclusion of the supply contract, inspections required by the IAEA for the continuity of safeguards will continue at the facilities not subject to the freeze.

3. When a significant portion of the LWR project is completed, but before delivery of key nuclear components, the DPRK will come into full compliance with its safeguards agreement with the IAEA (INFCIRC/403), including taking all steps that may be deemed necessary by the IAEA, following consultations with the Agency with regard to verifying the accuracy and completeness of the DPRK's initial report on all nuclear material in the DPRK.

_____

Robert L. Gallucci
Head of Delegation of the
United States of America,
Ambassador at Large of the
United States of America

_____

Kang, Sok Ju
Head of the Delegation of the
Democratic People's Republic of Korea,
First Vice-Minister of Foreign Affairs of the
Democratic People's Republic of Korea

APPENDIX E

TEXT OF PRESIDENT BILL CLINTON'S LETTER TO KIM JONG IL

20 October 1994

Excellency:

I wish to confirm to you that I will use the full powers of my office to facilitate arrangements for the financing and construction of a light-water nuclear power reactor project within the DPRK, and the funding and implementation of interim energy alternatives for the DPRK pending completion of the first reactor unit of the light-water reactor project. In addition, in the event that this reactor project is not completed for reasons beyond the control of the DPRK, I will use the full powers of my office to provide, to the extent necessary, such a project from the US, subject to approval of the US Congress. Similarly, in the event that the interim energy alternatives are not provided for reasons beyond the control of the DPRK, I will use the full powers of my office to provide, to the extent necessary, such interim energy alternatives from the US, subject to the approval of the US Congress.

I will follow this course of action so long as the DPRK continues to implement the policies described in the Agreed Framework between the United States of America and the Democratic People's Republic of Korea.

Sincerely,

Signed
Bill Clinton

His Excellency Kim Jong Il
Supreme Leader of the Democratic People's Republic of Korea
Pyongyang

APPENDIX F

KOREAN PENINSULA ENERGEY DEVELOPMENT ORGANIZATION-
DEMOCRATIC PEOPLE'S REPUBLIC OF KOREA
REACTOR SUPPLY AGREEMENT

15 December 1995

AGREEMENT ON SUPPLY OF A LIGHT-WATER REACTOR PROJECT TO THE
DEMOCRATIC PEOPLE'S REPUBLIC OF KOREA BETWEEN THE KOREAN PENINSULA
ENERGY DEVELOPMENT ORGANIZATION AND THE GOVERNMENT OF THE
DEMOCRATIC PEOPLE'S REPUBLIC OF KOREA

The Korean Peninsula Energy Development Organization (hereinafter referred to as "KEDO")
and the Government of the Democratic People's Republic of Korea (the Democratic People's
Republic of Korea is hereinafter referred to as the "DPRK"),

Recognizing that KEDO is an international organization to finance and supply a light-water
reactor project (hereinafter referred to as the "LWR project") to the DPRK as specified in the
Agreed Framework between the United States of America and the Democratic People's Republic
of Korea of October 21, 1994 (hereinafter referred to as the "US -DPRK Agreed Framework"),

Recognizing that the US -DPRK Agreed Framework and the June 13, 1995, US-DPRK Joint
Press Statement specify that the US will serve as the principal point of contact with the DPRK for
the LWR project, and

Reaffirming that the DPRK shall perform its obligations under the relevant provisions of the US -
DPRK Agreed Framework and shall accept the LWR project as specified in the June 13, 1995,
US-DPRK Joint Press Statement,

Have agreed as follows:

ARTICLE I--SCOPE OF SUPPLY
1. KEDO shall provide the LWR project, consisting of two pressurized light-water reactor (LWR)
units with two coolant loops and a generating capacity of approximately 1,000 megawatts each,
to the DPRK on a turnkey basis. The reactor model, selected by KEDO, will be the advanced
version of US-origin design and technology currently under production.

2. KEDO shall be responsible for the scope of supply for the LWR project, specified in Annex 1
to the Agreement. The DPRK shall be responsible for other tasks and items necessary for the
LWR project, specified in Annex 2 to the Agreement.

3. The project shall conform to a set of codes and standards equivalent to those of the IAEA and
the US and applied to the reactor model referred to in paragraph 1 of this Article. The set of
codes and standards shall apply to the design, manufacture, construction, testing, commissioning,
and operation and maintenance of the LWR plants, including safety, physical protection,
environmental protection, and storage and disposal of radioactive waste.

ARTICLE II--TERMS OF REPAYMENT
1. KEDO shall finance the cost of the tasks and items specified in Annex I to the Agreement to be
repaid by the DPRK on a long-term, interest-free basis.

2. The amount to be repaid by the DPRK will be jointly determined by KEDO and the DPRK
based on examination by each side of the technical description of the LWR project specified in

the commercial supply contract for the LWR project, the fair and reasonable market value of the LWR project, and the contract price payable by KEDO to its contractors and subcontractors under the commercial supply contracts for the tasks and items specified in Annex I to the Agreement. With respect to the tasks and items specified in Annex I to the Agreement, the DPRK shall not be responsible for any additional costs, other than those that result from actions by the DPRK or from its failure to take actions for which it is responsible, in which case the repayment amount shall be increased by an amount jointly determined by KEDO and the DPRK, based on actual added cost to the LWR project payable by KEDO.

3. The DPRK shall repay KEDO for each LWR plant in equal, semiannual installments, free of interest, over a 20-year term after completion of each LWR plant, including a three-year grace period beginning upon completion of that LWR plant. The DPRK may pay KEDO in cash, cash equivalents, or through the transfer of goods. In the event that the DPRK pays in cash equivalents or goods (such payment is hereinafter referred to as "in-kind payment"), the value of such in-kind payment shall be determined jointly by KEDO and the DPRK, based on an agreed formula for determining fair and reasonable market price.

4. Details concerning the amount and terms of repayment shall be specified in a separate protocol between KEDO and the DPRK pursuant to the Agreement.

ARTICLE III–DELIVERY SCHEDULE

1. KEDO shall develop a delivery schedule for the LWR project aimed at achieving a completion date of 2003. The schedule of relevant steps to be performed by the DPRK under the US-DPRK Agreed Framework, as specified in Annex 3 to the Agreement, shall be integrated with the delivery schedule for the LWR project with the aim of achieving the performance of such steps by 2003 and the smooth implementation of the LWR project. As specified in the US-DPRK Agreed Framework, the provision of the LWR project and the performance of the steps specified in Annex 3 to the Agreement are mutually conditional.

2. For purposes of the Agreement, "completion" of an LWR plant means completion of performance tests that is satisfactory in accordance with the set of codes and standards specified in Article I (3). Upon completion of each plant, the DPRK shall issue to KEDO a take-over certificate for each respective plant.

3. Details concerning the schedule for the delivery of the LWR project and the performance of the steps specified in Annex 3 to the Agreement, including mutually agreed procedures for any necessary changes and completion of a significant portion of the LWR project as specified in Annex 4 to the Agreement, shall be specified in a separate protocol between KEDO and the DPRK pursuant to the Agreement.

ARTICLE IV--IMPLEMENTING ARRANGEMENTS

1. The DPRK may designate a DPRK firm as its agent and authorize the firm to enter into implementing arrangements as necessary to facilitate the LWR project.

2. KEDO shall select a prime contractor to carry out the LWR project and shall conclude a commercial supply contract with this prime contractor. A US firm will serve as program coordinator to assist KEDO in supervising overall implementation of the LWR project, and KEDO will select the program coordinator.

3. KEDO and the DPRK shall facilitate practical arrangements that both sides deem necessary, including efficient contacts and cooperation among the participants in the LWR project, to ensure the expeditious and smooth implementation of the LWR project.

4. Written communications required for the implementation of the Agreement may be executed in the English or Korean language. Existing documents and data may be used or transmitted in their original languages.

5. KEDO, its contractors and subcontractors shall be permitted to operate offices at the project site and other directly related locations such as the nearby port or airport as shall be agreed between KEDO and the DPRK, as the progress of the LWR project may require.

6. The DPRK shall recognize KEDO's independent juridical status and shall accord KEDO and its staff such privileges and immunities in the territory of the DPRK as necessary to carry out the functions entrusted to KEDO. KEDO's juridical status and privileges and immunities shall be specified in a separate protocol between KEDO and the DPRK pursuant to the Agreement.

7. The DPRK shall take steps to protect the safety of all personnel sent to the DPRK by KEDO, its contractors and subcontractors, and their respective property. Appropriate consular protection in conformity with established international practice shall be allowed for all such personnel. Necessary consular arrangements shall be specified in a separate protocol between KEDO and the DPRK pursuant to the Agreement.

8. KEDO shall take steps to ensure that all personnel sent to the DPRK by KEDO, its contractors and subcontractors shall undertake to respect the relevant laws of the DPRK, as shall be agreed between KEDO and the DPRK, and to conduct themselves at all times in a decent and professional manner.

9. The DPRK shall not interfere with the repatriation, in accordance with customs clearance procedures, by KEDO, its contractors and subcontractors of construction equipment and remaining materials from the LWR project.

10. The DPRK shall seek recovery solely from the property and assets of KEDO for the satisfaction of any claims arising under the Agreement or from any of the acts and omissions, liabilities, or obligations of KEDO, its contractors and subcontractors in direct connection with the Agreement, protocols and contracts pursuant to the Agreement.

ARTICLE V--SITE SELECTION AND STUDY
1. KEDO shall conduct a study of the preferred Kumho area near Sinpo City, South Hamgyong Province to ensure that the site satisfies appropriate site selection criteria as shall be agreed between KEDO and the DPRK and to identify the requirements for construction and operation of the LWR plants, including infrastructure improvements.

2. To facilitate this study, the DPRK shall cooperate and provide KEDO with access to the relevant available information, including the results of the studies that were performed previously at this site. In the event that such data is not sufficient, KEDO shall make arrangements to obtain additional information or to conduct the necessary site studies.

3. Details concerning site access and the use of the site shall be specified in a separate protocol between KEDO and the DPRK pursuant to the Agreement.

ARTICLE VI--QUALITY ASSURANCE AND WARRANTIES
1. KEDO shall be responsible for design and implementation of a quality assurance program in accordance with the set of codes and standards specified in Article I(3). The quality assurance program shall include appropriate procedures for design, materials, manufacture and assembly of equipment and components, and quality of construction.

2. KEDO shall provide the DPRK with appropriate documentation on the quality assurance program, and the DPRK shall have the right to participate in the implementation of the quality

assurance program, which will include appropriate inspections, tests, commissioning, and review by the DPRK of the results thereof.

3. KEDO shall guarantee that the generating capacity of each LWR plant at the time of completion, as defined in Article III(2), will be approximately 1,000 megawatts. KEDO shall guarantee that the major components provided by relevant contractors and subcontractors will be new and free from defects in design, workmanship, and material for a period of two years after completion, but in no event longer than five years after the date of shipment of such major components. The LWR fuel for the initial loading for each LWR plant shall be guaranteed in accordance with standard nuclear industry practice. KEDO shall guarantee that the civil construction work for the LWR project will be free of defects in design, workmanship, and material for a period of two years after completion.

4. Details concerning the provisions of this Article and the content and procedures for issuance and receipt of warranties shall be specified in a separate protocol between KEDO and the DPRK pursuant to the Agreement.

ARTICLE VII--TRAINING
1. KEDO shall design and implement a comprehensive training program in accordance with standard nuclear industry practice for the DPRK's operation and maintenance of the LWR plants. Such training shall be held at mutually agreeable locations as soon as practicable. The DPRK shall be responsible for providing a sufficient number of qualified candidates for this program.

2. Details concerning the training program shall be specified in a separate protocol between KEDO and the DPRK pursuant to the Agreement.

ARTICLE VIII--OPERATION AND MAINTENANCE
1. KEDO shall assist the DPRK to obtain LWR fuel, other than that provided pursuant to Annex 1 to the Agreement, through commercial contracts with a DPRK-preferred supplier for the useful life of the LWR plants.

2. KEDO shall assist the DPRK to obtain spare and wear parts, consumables, special tools, and technical services for the operation and maintenance of the LWR plants, other than those provided pursuant to Annex 1 to the Agreement, through commercial contracts with a DPRK-preferred supplier for the useful life of the LWR plants.

3. KEDO and the DPRK shall cooperate to ensure the safe storage and disposition of the spent fuel from the LWR plants. If requested by KEDO, the DPRK shall relinquish any ownership rights over the LWR spent fuel and agree to the transfer of the spent fuel out of its territory as soon as technically possible after the fuel is discharged, through appropriate commercial contracts.

4. Necessary arrangements for the transfer of LWR spent fuel out of the DPRK shall be specified in a separate protocol between KEDO and the DPRK pursuant to the Agreement.

ARTICLE IX--SERVICES
1. The DPRK shall process for approval all applications necessary for completion of the LWR project expeditiously and free of charge. These approvals shall include all permits issued by the DPRK nuclear regulatory authority, customs clearance, entry and other permits, licenses, site access rights, and site take-over agreements. In the event that any such approval is delayed beyond the normally required time or denied, the DPRK shall notify KEDO promptly of the reasons therefor, and the schedule and cost for the LWR project may be adjusted as appropriate.

2. KEDO, its contractors and subcontractors, and their respective personnel shall be exempt from DPRK taxes, duties, charges and fees as shall be agreed between KEDO and the DPRK, and expropriation in connection with the LWR project.

3. All personnel sent to the DPRK by KEDO, its contractors and subcontractors shall be allowed unimpeded access to the project site and to appropriate and efficient transportation routes, including air and sea links, to and from the project site as designated by the DPRK and agreed between KEDO and the DPRK. Additional routes will be considered as the progress of the LWR project may require.

4. The DPRK shall, to 'the extent possible, make available at a fair price port services, transportation, labor, potable water, food, off-site lodging and offices, communications, fuel, electrical power, materials, medical services, currency exchanges and other financial services, and other amenities necessary for living and working by personnel sent to the DPRK by KEDO, its contractors and subcontractors.

5. KEDO, its contractors and subcontractors, and their respective personnel shall be allowed unimpeded use of available means of communications in the DPRK. In addition, KEDO, its contractors and subcontractors shall be permitted by the DPRK to establish secure and independent means of communications for their offices, based on a timely and case-by-case review of equipment requests and in accordance with relevant telecommunications regulations of the DPRK.

6. Details concerning the above-referenced services shall be specified, as appropriate, in one or more separate protocols between KEDO and the DPRK pursuant to the Agreement.

ARTICLE X--NUCLEAR SAFETY AND REGULATION
1. KEDO shall be responsible for assuring that design, manufacture, construction, testing, and commissioning of the LWR plants are in compliance with nuclear safety and regulatory codes and standards specified in Article I(3).

2. The DPRK shall issue a site take-over certificate to KEDO upon completion of the site survey. A construction permit shall be issued by the DPRK nuclear regulatory authority to KEDO, prior to the power block excavation, based on its review of the preliminary safety analysis report and the site studies and on its determination of whether the LWR project complies with the nuclear safety and regulatory codes and standards specified in Article I(3). A commissioning permit shall be issued by the DPRK nuclear regulatory authority to KEDO prior to initial fuel loading, based on its review of the final safety analysis report, which includes the as-built design of the LWR plant, and results of nonnuclear commissioning tests. KEDO shall provide the results of nuclear commissioning tests and operator-training records to the DPRK in support of its issuance of an operating permit to the operator. KEDO shall provide the DPRK, in a timely manner, with the safety analysis reports, necessary information including that on the codes and standards, and such other documents as KEDO deems necessary in order to make the required determination. The DPRK shall ensure that these permits will be issued in a timely manner not to impede the project schedule.

3. The DPRK shall be responsible for the safe operation and maintenance of the LWR plants, appropriate physical protection, environmental protection, and, consistent with Article VIII(3), the safe storage and disposal of radioactive waste, including spent fuel, in conformity with the set of codes and standards specified in Article I(3). In this regard, the DPRK shall assure that appropriate nuclear regulatory standards and procedures are in place to ensure the safe operation and maintenance of the LWR plants.

4. Prior to the shipment of any fuel assemblies to the DPRK, the DPRK shall observe the provisions set forth in the Convention on Nuclear Safety (done at Vienna, September 20, 1994), the Convention on Early Notification of a Nuclear Accident (adopted at Vienna, September 26, 1986), the Convention on Assistance in the Case of a Nuclear Accident or Radiological Emergency (adopted at Vienna, September 26, 1986), and the Convention on the Physical Protection of Nuclear Material (opened for signature at Vienna and New York, March 3, 1980).

5. After the completion of the LWR plants, KEDO and the DPRK shall conduct safety reviews to ensure the safe operation and maintenance of the LWR plants. In this regard, the DPRK shall provide necessary assistance to enable such reviews to be conducted as expeditiously as possible and shall give due consideration to the results of such reviews. Details concerning the schedule and procedures for conducting the safety reviews shall be specified in a separate protocol between KEDO and the DPRK pursuant to the Agreement.

6. In the event of a nuclear emergency or accident, the DPRK shall permit immediate access to the site and information by personnel sent by KEDO, its contractors and subcontractors to determine the extent of safety concerns and to provide safety assistance.

ARTICLE XI--NUCLEAR LIABILITY

1. The DPRK shall ensure that a legal and financial mechanism is available for meeting claims brought within the DPRK for damages in the event of a nuclear incident (as defined in the Vienna Convention on Civil Liability for Nuclear Damage, done at Vienna, May 21, 1963) in connection with the LWR plants. The legal mechanism shall include the channeling of liability in the event of a nuclear incident to the operator on the basis of absolute liability. The DPRK shall ensure that the operator is able to satisfy such liabilities.

2. Prior to the shipment of any fuel assemblies to the DPRK, the DPRK shall enter into an indemnity agreement with KEDO, and shall secure nuclear liability insurance or other financial security to protect KEDO, its contractors and subcontractors, and their respective personnel in connection with any third party claims in any court or forum arising from activities undertaken pursuant to the Agreement in the event of nuclear damage or loss occurring inside or outside the territory of the DPRK as a result of a nuclear incident in connection with the LWR plants. Details concerning the indemnity agreement and insurance or other financial security shall be specified in a separate protocol between KEDO and the DPRK pursuant to the Agreement.

3. The DPRK shall bring no claims against KEDO, its contractors and subcontractors, and their respective personnel arising out of any nuclear damage or loss.

4. This Article shall not be construed as acknowledging the jurisdiction of any court or forum or as waiving any immunity of either side.

5. The domestic legal system of the DPRK may provide that, if the operator proves that the nuclear damage resulted wholly or partly either from the gross negligence of the person suffering the damage or from an act or omission of such person done with intent to cause damage, the operator may be relieved wholly or partly from his obligation to pay compensation in respect of the damage suffered by such person. The operator shall have a right of recourse only if the damage caused by a nuclear incident results from an act or omission done with intent to cause damage, against the individual acting or omitting to act with such intent. For purposes of this paragraph, the terms "person" and "individual" shall have the same meaning as in the Vienna Convention on Civil Liability for Nuclear Damage (done at Vienna, May 21, 1963).

ARTICLE XII--INTELLECTUAL PROPERTY

1. In the course of performing its obligations under the Agreement, each side may receive, directly or indirectly, information relating to the intellectual property of the other side. All such

information and any materials or documents containing such information (collectively, the "Intellectual Property") are proprietary and confidential to such other side, whether or not protected by patent or copyright law. Each side agrees to protect the confidentiality of the other side's Intellectual Property and to use it only for the purposes of the LWR project as provided for in the Agreement and in accordance with international norms, including practices established by the Paris Convention on the Protection of Industrial Property Rights.

2. Except as otherwise agreed between the two sides, neither side shall replicate, copy, or otherwise reproduce any of the equipment or technology of the other side provided in connection with the LWR project.

ARTICLE XIII--ASSURANCES

1. The DPRK shall use the reactors, technology, and nuclear material (as defined in accordance with international practice) transferred pursuant to the Agreement, as well as any nuclear material used therein or produced through the use of such items, exclusively for peaceful, nonexplosive purposes.

2. The DPRK shall ensure that the reactors, technology, and nuclear material transferred pursuant to the Agreement, as well as any nuclear material used therein or produced through the use of such items, are used properly and exclusively for the purposes of the LWR project.

3. The DPRK shall provide effective physical protection in accordance with international standards with respect to the reactors and nuclear material transferred pursuant to the Agreement, as well as any nuclear material used therein or produced through the use of such items for the useful life of such reactors and nuclear material.

4. The DPRK shall apply IAEA safeguards to the reactors and nuclear material transferred pursuant to the Agreement, as well as any nuclear material used therein or produced through the use of such items, for the useful life of such reactors and nuclear material.

5. The DPRK shall at no time reprocess or increase the enrichment level of any nuclear material transferred pursuant to the Agreement, or any nuclear material used in or produced through the use of any reactor or nuclear material transferred in the LWR project.

6. The DPRK shall not transfer any nuclear equipment or technology or nuclear material transferred pursuant to the Agreement, or any nuclear material used therein or produced through the use of such items, outside the territory of the DPRK unless otherwise agreed between KEDO and the DPRK, except as provided for in Article VIII(3).

7. The above-referenced assurances may be supplemented by DPRK assurances, through appropriate arrangements, to KEDO members that provide to the DPRK any components controlled under the Export Trigger List of the Nuclear Suppliers Group for the LWR project, if and when such KEDO member or members and the DPRK deem it necessary.

ARTICLE XIV--FORCE MAJEURE

Either side's performance shall be considered excusably delayed if such delay is due to one or more events that are internationally accepted to constitute force majeure. Each such event is herein referred to as an event of "Force Majeure." The side whose performance is delayed by an event of Force Majeure shall provide notice of such delay to the other side promptly after such event has occurred and shall use such efforts as are reasonable in the circumstances to mitigate such delay and the effect thereof on such side's performance. The two sides shall then consult with each other promptly and in good faith to determine whether alternative performance and the adjustment of the schedule and cost of the LWR project are necessary.

ARTICLE XV--DISPUTE RESOLUTION

1. Any disputes arising out of the interpretation or implementation of the Agreement shall be settled through consultations between KEDO and the DPRK, in conformity with the principles of international law. KEDO and the DPRK shall organize a coordinating committee composed of three people from each side to help settle disputes that may arise in the process of implementing the Agreement.

2. Any dispute that cannot be resolved in this manner shall, at the request of either side and with the consent of the other side, be submitted to an arbitral tribunal composed as follows: KEDO and the DPRK shall each designate one arbitrator, and the two arbitrators so designated shall elect a third, who shall be the Chairman. If, within thirty days of the mutual agreement for arbitration, either KEDO or the DPRK has not designated an arbitrator, either KEDO or the DPRK may request the President of the International Court of Justice to appoint an arbitrator. The same procedure shall apply if, within thirty days of the designation or appointment of the second arbitrator, the third arbitrator has not been elected. A majority of the members of the arbitral tribunal shall constitute a quorum, and all decisions shall require the concurrence of two arbitrators. The arbitral procedure shall be fixed by the tribunal. The decisions of the tribunal shall be binding on KEDO and the DPRK. Each side shall bear the cost of its own arbitrator and its representation in the arbitral proceedings. The cost of the Chairman in discharging his duties and the remaining costs of the arbitral tribunal shall be borne equally by both sides.

ARTICLE XVI--ACTIONS IN THE EVENT OF NONCOMPLIANCE

1. KEDO and the DPRK shall perform their respective obligations in good faith to achieve the basic objectives of the Agreement.

2. In the event that either side fails to take its respective steps specified in the Agreement, the other side shall have the right to require the immediate payment of any amounts due and financial losses in connection with the LWR project.

3. In the event of late payment or nonpayment by either side with respect to financial obligations to the other side incurred in implementing the Agreement, the other side shall have the right to assess and apply penalties against that side. Details concerning the assessment and application of such penalties shall be specified in a separate protocol between KEDO and the DPRK pursuant to the Agreement.

ARTICLE XVII--AMENDMENTS

1. The Agreement may be amended by written agreement between the two sides.

2. Any amendment shall enter into force on the date of its signature.

ARTICLE XVIII--ENTRY INTO FORCE

1. The Agreement shall constitute an international agreement between KEDO and the DPRK, and shall be binding on both sides under international law.

2. The Agreement shall enter into force on the date of its signature.

3. The Annexes to the Agreement shall be an integral part of the Agreement.

4. The protocols pursuant to the Agreement shall enter into force on the date of their respective signature.

IN WITNESS WHEREOF, the undersigned, being duly authorized, have signed the Agreement.

DONE at New York City on this 15th day of December, 1995, in duplicate in the English language.

For the Korean Peninsula Energy Development Organization

Stephen W. Bosworth	Ho Jong
Ambassador-at-Large	For the Government of the DPRK
Executive Director KEDO	Ministry of Foreign Affairs DPRK

Annex 1

The scope of supply of the LWR plants referenced in Article I of the Agreement for which KEDO shall be responsible shall consist of the following tasks and items:

1. Site survey.

2. Site preparation, which shall consist of clearing and leveling of the site and provision of electricity necessary for construction at the site and water services at the site necessary for completion of the LWR plants.

3. Preconstruction infrastructure that KEDO deems is integral to and exclusively for use in the construction of the LWR plants, which shall consist of roads within the site boundary, access roads from the site to off-site roads, barge docking facilities and a road from there to the site, a waterway and water catchment facilities including weir, and housing and related facilities for KEDO, its contractors and subcontractors.

4. Technical documents necessary for the operation and maintenance of the LWR plants, including the construction schedule.

5. Power plant systems, facilities, buildings, structures, equipment, and auxiliary facilities, including laboratory and measurement equipment and cold machine shop, that KEDO deems necessary for the two LWR plants.

6. A low and medium radioactive waste storage building with a ten-year storage capacity for the two LWR plants.

7. All tests required up to take-over.

8. The inventory of spare parts, wear parts, consumables, and special tools as KEDO deems necessary for a two-year period of plant operation, in accordance with standard nuclear industry practice.

9. Nuclear fuel for the initial loading of each LWR, including such fuel rods as may be necessary to preserve safety for initial operation.

10. A comprehensive training program for the operation and maintenance of the LWR plants implemented by KEDO and its contractors in accordance with standard nuclear industry practice, including provision of a full-scope simulator.

11. Technical support services as KEDO deems necessary for operation and maintenance of the first LWR plant for one year after completion of that LWR plant, in accordance with standard nuclear industry practice.

12. Overall project management.

The tasks and items referenced in Article I(2) of the Agreement for which the DPRK shall be responsible shall consist of the following:

1. Securing the site (land and marine) for the LWR project, including relocation of population, existing structures and facilities.

2. Provision of/access to information and documents necessary for implementation of the LWR project available in the DPRK.

3. Stable supply of electricity for commissioning of the two LWR plants as available in the DPRK.

4. Access to existing harbor, rail, and airport facilities designated by the DPRK and agreed between KEDO and the DPRK in the vicinity of the site for the transportation of materials and equipment necessary for the LWR project.

5. Securing aggregate and quarry site.

6. Communication lines to the LWR project site, to the extent possible, pursuant to Article IX of the Agreement.

7. Qualified operators trained by KEDO to participate in the commissioning.

Annex 3

The relevant steps to be performed by the DPRK in connection with the supply of the LWR project under the US-DPRK Agreed Framework, as referenced in Article III(1) of the Agreement, consist of the following:

1. The DPRK will remain a party to the Treaty on the Non-Proliferation of Nuclear Weapons and will allow implementation of its safeguards agreement under the Treaty, as specified in the US-DPRK Agreed Framework.

2. The DPRK will continue the freeze on its graphite-moderated reactors and related facilities and provide full cooperation to the IAEA in its monitoring of the freeze.

3. The DPRK will refrain from the construction of new graphite-moderated reactors and related facilities.

4. In the event that US firms will be providing any key nuclear components, the US and the DPRK will conclude a bilateral agreement for peaceful nuclear cooperation prior to the delivery of such components. Such agreement will not be implemented until a significant portion of the LWR project is completed, as specified in Annex 4 to the Agreement. For purposes of the Agreement, "key nuclear components" are the components controlled under the Export Trigger List of the Nuclear Suppliers Group.

5. The DPRK will continue cooperation on safe storage and ultimate disposition of spent fuel from the 5-megawatt experimental reactor.

6. Upon the signing of the Agreement, the DPRK will permit resumption of ad hoc and routine inspections under the DPRK's safeguards agreement with the IAEA with respect to facilities not subject to the freeze.

7. When a significant portion of the LWR project is completed, but before delivery of key nuclear components, the DPRK will come into full compliance with its IAEA safeguards agreement, including taking all steps that may be deemed necessary by the IAEA.

8. When the first LWR plant is completed, the DPRK will begin dismantlement of its frozen graphite-moderated reactors and related facilities, and will complete such dismantlement when the second LWR plant is completed.

9. When delivery of the key nuclear components for the first LWR plant begins, the transfer from the DPRK of spent fuel from the 5-megawatt experimental reactor for ultimate disposition will begin and will be completed when the first LWR plant is completed.

Annex 4

A significant portion of the LWR project, referenced in Article III(3) of the Agreement, means the following. A further elaboration of the definition will be specified in the separate protocol referenced in Article III(3).

1. Conclusion of the contract for the LWR project.

2. Completion of site preparation, excavation, and completion of facilities necessary to support construction of the LWR project.

3. Completion of initial plant design for the selected site.

4. Specification and fabrication of major reactor components for the first LWR unit as provided for in project plans and schedules.

5. Delivery of essential nonnuclear components for the first LWR unit, including turbines and generators, according to project plans and schedules.

6. Construction of the turbine buildings and other auxiliary buildings for the first LWR unit, to the stage provided for in project plans and schedules.

7. Construction of the reactor building and containment structure for the first LWR unit to the point suitable for the introduction of components of the Nuclear Steam Supply System.

8. Civil construction and fabrication and delivery of components for the second LWR unit according to project plans and schedules.

APPENDIX G

TREATY ON THE NONPROLIFERATION OF NUCLEAR WEAPONS

5 March 1970

The States concluding this Treaty, hereinafter referred to as the "Parties to the Treaty,"

Considering the devastation that would be visited upon all mankind by a nuclear war and the consequent need to make every effort to avert the danger of such a war and to take measures to safeguard the security of peoples,

Believing that the proliferation of nuclear weapons would seriously enhance the danger of nuclear war.

In conformity with resolutions of the United Nations General Assembly calling for the conclusion of an agreement on the prevention of wider dissemination of nuclear weapons,

Undertaking to co-operate in facilitating the application of International Atomic Energy Agency safeguards on peaceful nuclear activities,

Expressing their support for research, development and other efforts to further the application, within the framework of the International Atomic Energy Agency safeguards system, of the principle of safeguarding effectively the flow of source and special fissionable materials by use of instruments and other techniques at certain strategic points,

Affirming the principle that the benefits of peaceful applications of nuclear technology, including any technological by-products which may be derived by nuclear-weapon States from the development of nuclear explosive devices, should be available for peaceful purposes to all Parties to the Treaty, whether nuclear-weapon or nonnuclear-weapon States,

Convinced that, in furtherance of this principle, all Parties to the Treaty are entitled to participate in the fullest possible exchange of scientific information for, and to contribute alone or in co-operation with other States to the further development of the applications of atomic energy for peaceful purposes,

Declaring their intention to achieve at the earliest possible date the cessation of the nuclear race and to undertake effective measures in the direction of nuclear disarmament,

Urging the co-operation of all States in the attainment of this objective,

Recalling the determination expressed by the Parties to the 1963 Treaty banning nuclear weapon tests in the atmosphere, in outer space and underwater in its Preamble to seek to achieve the discontinuance of all test explosions of nuclear weapons for all time and to continue negotiations to this end,

Desiring to further the easing of international tension and the strengthening of trust between States in order to facilitate the cessation of the manufacture of nuclear weapons, the liquidation of all their existing stockpiles, and the elimination from national arsenals of nuclear weapons and the means of their delivery pursuant to a Treaty on general and complete disarmament under strict and effective international control,

Recalling that, in accordance with the Charter of the United Nations, States must refrain in their international relations from the threat or use of force against the territorial integrity or political independence of any State, or in any other manner inconsistent with the Purposes of the United Nations, and that the establishment and maintenance of international peace and security are to be promoted with the least diversion for armaments of the world's human and economic resources,

Have agreed as follows:

Article I

Each nuclear-weapon State Party to the Treaty undertakes not to transfer to any recipient whatsoever nuclear weapons or other nuclear explosive devices or control over such weapons or explosive devices directly, or indirectly; and not in any way to assist, encourage, or induce any nonnuclear-weapon State to manufacture or otherwise acquire nuclear weapons or other nuclear explosive devices, or control over such weapons or explosive devices.

Article II

Each nonnuclear-weapon State Party to the Treaty undertakes not to receive the transfer from any transfer or whatsoever of nuclear weapons or other nuclear explosive devices or of control over such weapons or explosive devices directly, or indirectly; not to manufacture or otherwise acquire nuclear weapons or other nuclear explosive devices; and not to seek or receive any assistance in the manufacture of nuclear weapons or other nuclear explosive devices.

Article III

Each nonnuclear-weapon State Party to the Treaty undertakes to accept safeguards, as set forth in an agreement to be negotiated and concluded with the International Atomic Energy Agency in accordance with the Statute of the International Atomic Energy Agency and the Agency's safeguards system, for the exclusive purpose of verification of the fulfillment of its obligations assumed under this Treaty with a view to preventing diversion of nuclear energy from peaceful uses to nuclear weapons or other nuclear explosive devices. Procedures for the safeguards required by this Article shall be followed with respect to source or special fissionable material whether it is being produced, processed or used in any principal nuclear facility or is outside any such facility. The safeguards required by this Article shall be applied on all source or special fissionable material in all peaceful nuclear activities within the territory of such State, under its jurisdiction, or carried out under its control anywhere.

Each State Party to the Treaty undertakes not to provide: source or special fissionable material, or equipment or material especially designed or prepared for the processing, use or production of special fissionable material, to any nonnuclear-weapon State for peaceful purposes, unless the source or special fissionable material shall be subject to the safeguards required by this Article. The safeguards required by this Article shall be implemented in a manner designed to comply with Article IV of this Treaty, and to avoid hampering the economic or technological development of the Parties or international co-operation in the field of peaceful nuclear activities, including the international exchange of nuclear material and equipment for the processing, use or production of nuclear material for peaceful purposes in accordance with the provisions of this Article and the principle of safeguarding set forth in the Preamble of the Treaty.

Non-nuclear-weapon States Party to the Treaty shall conclude agreements with the International Atomic Energy Agency to meet the requirements of this Article either individually or together with other States in accordance with the Statute of the International Atomic Energy Agency. Negotiation of such agreements shall commence within 180 days from the original entry into force of this Treaty. For States depositing their instruments of ratification or accession after the 180-day period, negotiation of such agreements shall commence not later than the date of such deposit. Such agreements shall enter into force not later than eighteen months after the date of initiation of negotiations.

Article IV

Nothing in this Treaty shall be interpreted as affecting the inalienable right of all the Parties to the Treaty to develop research, production and use of nuclear energy for peaceful purposes without discrimination and unconformity with Articles I and II of this Treaty.

All the Parties to the Treaty undertake to facilitate, and have the right to participate in, the fullest possible exchange of equipment, materials and scientific and technological information for the peaceful uses of nuclear energy. Parties to the Treaty in a position to do so shall also co-operate in contributing alone or together with other States or international organizations to the further development of the applications of nuclear energy for peaceful purposes, especially in the territories of nonnuclear-weapon States Party to the Treaty, with due consideration for the needs of the developing areas of the world.

Article V

Each Party to the Treaty undertakes to take appropriate measures to ensure that, in accordance with this Treaty, under appropriate international observation and through appropriate international procedures, potential benefits from any peaceful applications of nuclear explosions will be made available to nonnuclear-weapon States Party to the Treaty on a nondiscriminatory basis and that the charge to such Parties for the explosive devices used will be as low as possible and exclude any charge for research and development. Non-nuclear-weapon States Party to the Treaty shall be able to obtain such benefits, pursuant to a special international agreement or agreements, through an appropriate international body with adequate representation of nonnuclear-weapon States. Negotiations on this subject shall commence as soon as possible after the Treaty enters into force. Non-nuclear-weapon States Party to the Treaty so desiring may also obtain such benefits pursuant to bilateral agreements.

Article VI

Each of the Parties to the Treaty undertakes to pursue negotiations in good faith on effective measures relating to cessation of the nuclear arms race at an early date and to nuclear disarmament, and on a treaty on general and complete disarmament under strict and effective international control.

Article VII

Nothing in this Treaty affects the right of any group of States to conclude regional treaties in order to assure the total absence of nuclear weapons in their respective territories.

Article VIII

Any Party to the Treaty may propose amendments to this Treaty. The text of any proposed amendment shall be submitted to the Depositary Governments, which shall circulate it to all Parties to the Treaty. Thereupon, if requested to do so by one-third or more of the Parties to the Treaty, the Depositary Governments shall convene a conference, to which they shall invite all the Parties to the Treaty, to consider such an amendment.

Any amendment to this Treaty must be approved by a majority of the votes of all the Parties the Treaty, including the votes of all nuclear-weapon States Party to the Treaty and all other Parties which, on the date the amendment is circulated, are members of the Board of Governors of the International Atomic Energy Agency. The amendment shall enter into force for each Party that deposits its instrument of ratification of the amendment upon the deposit of such instruments of ratification by a majority of all the Parties, including the instruments of ratification of all nuclear-weapon States Party to the Treaty and all other Parties which, on the date the amendment is circulated, are members of the Board of Governors of the International Atomic Energy Agency. Thereafter, it shall enter into force for any other Party upon the deposit of its instrument of ratification of the amendment.

Five years after the entry into force of this Treaty, a conference of Parties to the Treaty shall be held in Geneva, Switzerland, in order to review the operation of this Treaty with a view to assuring that the purposes of the Preamble and the provisions of the Treaty are being realized. At intervals of five years thereafter, a majority of the Parties to the Treaty may obtain, by submitting a proposal to this effect to the Depositary Governments, the convening of further conferences with the same objective of reviewing the operation of the Treaty.

Article IX
This Treaty shall be open to all States for signature. Any State which does not sign the Treaty before its entry into force in accordance with paragraph 3 of this Article may accede to it at any time.

This Treaty shall be subject to ratification by signatory States. Instruments of ratification and instruments of accession shall be deposited with the Governments of the United Kingdom of Great Britain and Northern Ireland, the Union of Soviet Socialist Republics and the United States of America, which are hereby designated the Depositary Governments.

This Treaty shall enter into force after its ratification by the States, the Governments of which are designated Depositaries of the Treaty, and forty other States signatory to this Treaty and the deposit of their instruments of ratification. For the purposes of this Treaty, a nuclear-weapon State is one, which has manufactured and exploded a nuclear weapon or other nuclear explosive device prior to 1 January 1967.

For States whose instruments of ratification or accession are deposited subsequent to the entry into force of this Treaty, it shall enter into force on the date of the deposit of their instruments of ratification or accession.

The Depositary Governments shall promptly inform all signatory and acceding States of the date of each signature, the date of deposit of each instrument of ratification or of accession, the date of the entry into force of this Treaty, and the date of receipt of any requests for convening a conference or other notices.

This Treaty shall be registered by the Depositary Governments pursuant to Article 102 of the Charter of the United Nations.

Article X
1. Each party shall in exercising its national sovereignty have the right to withdraw from the Treaty if it decides that extraordinary events, related to the subject matter of this Treaty, have jeopardized the supreme interests of its country. It shall give notice of such withdrawal to all other Parties to the Treaty and to the United Nations Security Council three months in advance. Such notice shall include a statement of the extraordinary events it regards as having jeopardized its supreme interests.

2. Twenty-five years after the entry into force of the Treaty, a conference shall be convened to decide whether the Treaty shall continue in force indefinitely, or shall be extended for an

additional fixed period or periods. This decision shall be taken by a majority of the Parties to the Treaty.

Article XI
This Treaty, the English, Russian, French, Spanish and Chinese texts of which are equally authentic, shall be deposited in the archives of the Depositary Governments. Duly certified copies of this Treaty shall be transmitted by the Depositary Governments to the Governments of the signatory and acceding States.

In witness whereof the undersigned, duly authorized, have signed this Treaty.

Done in triplicate, at the cities of London, Moscow and Washington, the first day of July, one thousand nine hundred and sixty-eight.

GLOSSARY

Betatron. A machine used to accelerate electrons to energies of up to 300 mega-electron volts in pulsed output. The electrons move in an orbit of constant radius between the poles of an electromagnet, and a rapidly alternating magnetic field provides the means of acceleration.

B-25 Betatron. A piece of equipment that permits the study of internal structures of material with the help of beta-radiation at an energy level of 25 mega-electron volts (Kaurov 2000, 17).

Denuclearization. An action that prohibits, prevents, or eliminates a nation's capability to possess or produce nuclear weapons.

Graphite-moderated reactor. Gas-cooled graphite-moderated reactors (GCR) are directly an outgrowth of the early nuclear weapons programs. In the late 1940's and early 1950's the United States, former Soviet Union, Great Britain, and France, seeking to develop their own nuclear bombs, focused their reactor development on the GCR, a relatively good producer of weapons-grade plutonium that is fueled with natural uranium (Colliers Encyclopedia 1995, s.v. "Nuclear power").

International Atomic Energy Agency (IAEA). A United Nations organization that was established in 1957 and is headquartered in Vienna, Austria. It is an intergovernmental organization established to seek to accelerate and enlarge the contributions of atomic energy to peace, health, and prosperity throughout the world. It assists member nations, especially developing countries, by providing facilities and fellowships for training in nuclear science and technology and by making available the services of experts and essential items of equipment. The IAEA also arranges for the supply of nuclear materials and reactors, finances research projects, and acts as a central agency for the diffusion of information on the peaceful uses of atomic energy. In the field of disarmament, the IAEA plays an important policing role concerning the treaty on the nonproliferation of nuclear weapons, which went into effect in 1970. In this role, the IAEA's purpose is to insure that developing nations do not use their civilian nuclear power plants as a foundation for a nuclear weapons program. The IAEA conducts ad hoc and regular inspections of nuclear power plants to insure that weapons-grade plutonium has not been diverted from fuel cells.

K-60,000 cobalt installation. A piece of equipment that allows various materials to be exposed to gamma radiation of the Cobalt-60 isotope with a power equivalent to 60 kg of radium (Kaurov 2000, 17).

Korean Electric Power Corporation (KEPCO). A South Korean energy company designated by KEDO on 12 June 1995 to serve as the principal contractor responsible to provide the DPRK with two light-water reactors.

Korean Peninsula Energy Development Organization (KEDO). An international organization established on 9 March 1995 to advance the implementation of the essential provisions of the Agreed Framework.

Light-water reactor (LWR). A nuclear reactor that is light-water cooled and moderated and is fueled by enriched uranium. There are two principal types of light-water reactors: the

111

boiling-water reactor (BWR) and the pressurized-water reactor (PWR). In the BWR, steam entering the electrical turbine generator is produced directly in the reactor core, whereas a PWR uses steam generators to separate the light-water coolant in the reactor from the steam flowing to the turbine (Kihl and Hayes 1997, 17).

Moderator. A substance that slows neutrons as they pass from one fuel rod to another. The moderator fills the space between the fuel rods in the fuel assemblies. Slow neutrons are needed for fission (The World Book Encyclopedia 1999).

Missile Technology Control Regime (MTCR). An informal international political arrangement designed to control the proliferation of rocket and unmanned air vehicle systems (and their associated equipment and technology) capable of delivering weapons of mass destruction. Formed in 1987, it has since been expanded to include 33 member countries. The regime controls are applicable to such rocket and unmanned air vehicles as ballistic missiles, space launch vehicles, sounding rockets, unmanned air vehicles, cruise missiles, drones and remotely piloted vehicles capable of delivering a 500 kilogram (1102 lb.) payload at least 300 kilometers (186 miles).

Nonproliferation Treaty (NPT). A 1970 international treaty established by the United Nations to prevent the spread of nuclear weapons and weapons technology, foster the peaceful uses of nuclear energy, and further the goal of achieving general and complete disarmament. The treaty established a safeguards system under the responsibility of the IAEA, which also plays a central role under the treaty in areas of technology transfer for peaceful purposes. Today there are 187 signatory nations.

Nuclear nonproliferation. Refers to the goal of preventing the spread of nuclear weapons and related technologies to nations and groups that currently do not possess them.

Nuclear warhead. An item which normally consists of the explosive system, the nuclear system, and electrical circuitry. It may be of an implosion type, gun-type, or thermonuclear type. It is usually designed to be mounted in a missile or projectile (Technical Publication 4-1).

Nuclear weapon. A complete assembly (i.e., implosion type, gun-type, or thermonuclear type), in its intended ultimate configuration which, upon completion of the prescribed arming, fusing, and firing sequence, is capable of producing the intended nuclear reaction and release of energy (JP 3-12).

Proliferation. The process by which one nation after another comes into possession of or into the right to determine the use of nuclear weapons, each potentially able to launch a nuclear attack upon another nation (JP 1-02).

Warhead. The part of the missile, projectile, torpedo, rocket, or other munitions which contains either the nuclear or thermonuclear system (JP 1-02).

Weapon of Mass Destruction. In this discussion refers to nuclear explosives, radiological, biological or chemical weapons

REFERENCE LIST

Anderson, Desaix. 2001. *Myths of KEDO.* Washington DC: Georgetown-Pacific Century Institute. Database. Available from http://www.kedo.org/myths.htm. Internet accessed on 11 August 2001.

Andrianov, Vladimir D. 2000. *Economics aspects of the North Korean nuclear program.* Pg. 41-50. Edited by James Clay Moltz and Alexandre Y. Mansourov. *The North Korea nuclear program: Security, strategy, and new perspectives from Russia.* NY: Routledge.

Atomic Energy Act of 1954. Statutes at Large. 1954. Chap. 1073, sec. 1-291.

Bandow, Doug. 1993. *North Korea and the risks of coercive nonproliferation.* Database. Available from http://www.cato.org/ pubs/fpbriefs/fpb-024.html. Internet accessed on 11 November 2001.

Berry Jr., William E. 1995. *North Korea's nuclear program: The Clinton administration's response.* Colorado Springs, CO: USAF Academy, Institute for National Security Studies.

Boose Jr., Donald W. 1996. *Conference Report: International workshop on the US-ROK alliance.* Carlisle Barracks, PA: US Army War College, Strategic Studies Institute (SSI).

Bush, George W. 2002. *The President's state of the union address.* Washington, DC: The White House. Database. Available from http://www.whitehouse.gov. Internet. Accessed on 11 March 2002.

Cheney, Richard B. 1991. Cheney to Israel: Thanks for destroying Iraqi reactor; will US take 10 years to accept Israeli stance on peace? Publications of the Center for Security Policy No. 91-P 110. *The Center for Security Policy.* Washington, DC: Publications of the Center for Security Policy. Database. Available from http:// http://www.security-policy.org/papers/1991/91-P110.html Internet. Accessed on 11 January 2002.

Clinton, William. 2000. *A National security strategy for a global age.* Washington, DC: The White House.

Central Intelligence Agency. 2002. *The World Factbook--Korea, North.* Washington DC: Central Intelligence Agency. Database. Available from http://www.cia.gov/cia/publications/factbook/geos/ kn.html. Internet. Accessed on 11 March 2002.

Committee on International Security and Arms Control of the National Academy of Sciences. 1994. Making a bomb using plutonium from a power reactor. Pg. 32-33. In *Management and disposition of excess weapons plutonium.* National Academy Press. Database. Available from http://www.ccnr.org/reactor_plute.html. Internet. Accessed on 7 March 2002.

Council for Nuclear Fuel Cycle, Institute for Energy Economics, Japan. 2001. *Can reactor grade plutonium produce nuclear fission weapons?* Database. Available from http://www.cnfc.or.jp/reports/rep0105e.html. Internet. Accessed on 7 March 2002.

113

Denisov, Valery I. 2000. *Nuclear institution and organizations in North Korea.* Pg. 21-26. Edited by James Clay Moltz and Alexandre Y. Mansourov. *The North Korea nuclear program: Security, strategy, and new perspectives from Russia.* NY: Routledge.

Dingman, Roger. 1988. Atomic diplomacy during the Korean War. *International Security,* 13, no. 3 (winter): 60-86.

Ekeus, Rolf. 1991. United Nations Security Council. Report S/23165, Annex: Report by the Executive Chairman of the Special Commission established by the Secretary-General pursuant to paragraph 9(b)(i) of Security Council resolution 687. (25 October 1991).

Gallucci, Robert L. 1995. *95/02/23 Testimony: R. Gallucci on US-DPRK Agreed Framework Bureau of Political Military Affairs.* Washington DC: US Department of State. Database. Available from http://dosfan.lib.uic.edu/ERC/bureaus/eap/ 950223GallucciUSDPRK.html. Internet. Accessed on 11 August 2001.

Gaffney, Frank. 1993. What to do about North Korea's nuclear threat: Execute the 'Osirak' remedy. *Publications of the Center for Security Policy.* Database. Available from http://www.security-policy.org/papers/1993/93-D20.html. Internet. Accessed on 12 Jan 2002.

George, Alexander, and Richard Smoke. 1974. *Deterrence in American foreign policy, theory and practice.* NY: Columbia University Press.

Gilinsky, Victor. 2000. Plutonium from US-supplied LWRs for North Korea: Do we have to worry about it? Speech delivered at the *Forum on Promoting International Scientific, Technological and Economic Cooperation in the Korean Peninsula: Enhancing Stability and International Dialogue*, 1-2 June 2000, in cooperation with *Istituto Diplomatico* and 'Mario Toscano.' Rome, Italy: Villa Madama. Database. Available from http://www.npec-web.org/essay/6-4-00-DPRK-Gilinsky.htm. Internet. Accessed on 28 March 2002.

Hahn, Ho Suk. 2000. *The US-DPRK relations at the close of the 20th century and the prospects for united Korea at the dawn of the 21st century, Part 1: American nuclear threats and North Korea's counter strategy.* Database. Available from http://kimsoft.com/2000/hanho.htm. Internet. Accessed on 27 October 2001.

Henriksen, Thomas H., and Mo Jongryn. 1997. *North Korea after Kim Il Sung: Continuity or change?* Stanford CA: Stanford University, Hoover Institute Press.

Holdren John P. 1989. Civilian Nuclear Technologies and Nuclear Weapons Proliferation. Pg. 161-198. In *New technologies and the arms race.* NY: St. Martin's Press.

Hubbard, Thomas C., Ambassador to the Republic of Korea. 2001. Korea of the future: An update on US-Korean relations, new economic opportunities, Korea in the Asian region. Speech delivered for *the International Relations Council and the Korea Economic Institute,* 13 December 2001, in cooperation with the University of Kansas, the Korean-American Society of Greater Kansas City and the World Trade Center of the Greater Kansas City Chamber of Commerce. Kansas City Missouri: The Westin Crown Center.

International Atomic Energy Agency. 1994. *Convention on nuclear safety.* Vienna, Austria: Information Circular/449.

Kahan, Jerome H. 1994. *Nuclear Threats from small states*. Carlisle, PA: US Army War College, Strategic Studies Institute (SSI).

Kanter, Arnold, and Joel Wit. 1998. The Future of the Agreed Framework. Database. Available from http://www.nyu.edu/globalbeat/asia/ Kanter111798.html. Internet. Accessed on 11 January 2002.

Kaurov, Georgiy. 2000. A technical history of Soviet-North Korean nuclear relations. Pg. 15-20. Edited by James Clay Moltz and Alexandre Y. Mansourov. *The North Korea nuclear program: Security, strategy, and new perspectives from Russia.* NY: Routledge.

Kay, David A. 1995. Denial and Deception Practices of WMD Proliferators: Iraq and Beyond. *The Washington Quarterly* (winter): 85.

Kihl, Young Whan, and Peter Hayes. 1997. *Peace and security in northeast Asia: The nuclear issue and the Korean peninsula.* Armonk, NY, and London, England: An East Gate Book.

Mark, J. Carson. 1993. Explosive properties of reactor-grade plutonium. *Science and Global Security*. 4: 111-128.

Martin, Curtis H. 1999. Lessons of the Agreed Framework for using engagement as a nonproliferation tool. *The Nonproliferation Review* (fall): 35-50.

Masao, Okonogi. 1995. Assessing the US-North Korea agreement. *Joint Forces Quarterly* (spring): 23-25.

Maxon, Richard G. 1995. Nature's eldest law: A survey of a nation's right to act in self-defense. *Parameters* 25, no. 3 (autumn): 55-68.

Mazarr, Michael J. 1995. *North Korea and the bomb: A case study in nonproliferation*. NY: St. Martin's Press, Scholarly and Reference Division.

Milioti, Stephen J., Kang Young Chol, and Brian Kremer. 2001. *KEDO's nuclear safety approach*. NY: KEDO.

Ministry of National Defense, Republic of Korea. 1998. *Defense White Paper*. Seoul, Korea: Ministry of National Defense. Database. Available from http://www.mnd.go.kr/mnden/ sub_menu/w_book/1998/ref/appendix17.htm Internet. Accessed on 30 March 2002.

_____. 2000. *Defense White Paper*. Seoul, Korea: Ministry of National Defense.

Minnich, James M. 2001. *ROK and DPRK energy sectors: Current statuses and plans for the future*. Database. Available from http://www.faoa.org. Internet. Accessed on 15 February 2002.

Moltz, James Clay, and Alexandre Y. Mansourov, eds. 2000. *The North Korea nuclear program: security, strategy, and new perspectives from Russia*. NY: Routledge.

Moltz, James Clay. 2000. Russia, North Korea, and the US Policy toward the Nuclear Crisis. Pg. 1-12. Edited by James Clay Moltz and Alexandre Y. Mansourov. *The North Korea nuclear program: Security, strategy, and new perspectives from Russia.* NY: Routledge.

Muller, Harald, David Fisher, and Wolfgang Kotter. 1994. *Nuclear non-proliferation and global order.* London: Oxford University Press.

National Intelligence Council, and the Federal Research Division of the Library of Congress. 2001. *North Korea's engagement--Perspectives, outlook, and implications.* Washington DC: Central Intelligence Agency. Database. Available from http://www.cia.gov/nic/pubs/ conference_reports/nk_conference.html. Internet. Accessed on 14 December 2001.

Niksch, Larry. 1995. *The agreed framework: View from Washington.* Prepared for *the International Workshop on the US-ROK Alliance, 5-7 October 1995,* organized by the Institute for Far Eastern Studies of Kyungnam University and the Strategic Studies Institute of the US Army War College in partnership with the US Defense Nuclear Agency and the Korea Society. Seoul, Korea: the Ritz-Carlton Hotel.

Nuclear Nonproliferation Act. U.S. Code. 1978. Vol. 1, sec 129.

Oberdorfer, Don. 1997. *The Two Koreas: A Contemporary History.* Indianapolis, IN: Basic Books.

Ono, Masaaki. 1999. *KEDO as a security institution: A firsthand report. Japan Echo* 26, No. 5, (5 October). Journal on-line. Available from http://www.japanecho.co.jp/ docs/html260513.html. Internet. Accessed on 6 August 2001.

Perry, William J. 1999. *Review of United States policy toward North Korea: Findings and recommendations.* Washington DC: State Department. Database. Available from http://www.state.gov/www/regions/eap/991012_northkorea_rpt.html. Internet. Accessed on 14 December 2001.

Pike, John. 2001. WMD Around the World, North Korea. *Federation of American Scientist.* Washington, DC: Federation of American Scientists. Database. Available from http://www.fas.org/ nuke/guide/dprk/facility/index.html. Internet. Accessed on 11 January 2002.

Plunk, Daryl. 2001. The new US administration and North Korea policy. Pg. 15-23. Edited by National Intelligence Council and the Federal Research Division of the Library of Congress. 2001. *North Korea's engagement--Perspectives, outlook, and implications.* Washington DC: Central Intelligence Agency. Database. Available from http://www.cia. gov/nic/pubs/conference_reports/ nk_conference.html. Internet. Accessed on 14 December 2001.

Pollack, Jonathan D., and Lee Chung Min. 1999. *Preparing for Korean unification: scenarios & implications.* Santa Monica, CA: RAND.

Reese, David. 1998. *The prospect for North Korea's survival.* Oxford, NY: Oxford University Press, International Institute for Strategic Studies.

Reiss, Mitchell. 1995. *Bridled ambition.* Washington, DC: The Woodrow Wilson Center Press.

Roberson, Brad, Sergeant First Class who conducted MIA remains recovery in the DPRK from June to July 2000. Interview by author, August 2000. Papers are located in author's desk.

Savada, Andrea Matles. 1993. *North Korea: A country study.* Washington DC: Federal Research Division, Library of Congress.

Schneider, Barry R. 1995. *Radical responses to radical regimes: Evaluating preemptive counter-proliferation.* Washington, DC: Institute for National Strategic Studies, National Defense University.

Sigal, Leon V. 1998. *Disarming strangers: Nuclear diplomacy with North Korea.* Princeton, NJ: Princeton University Press.

Sokolski, Henry D. 2001. *Planning for a peaceful Korea.* Carlisle, PA: US Army War College, Strategic Studies Institute (SSI).

Sokolski, Henry D., and Victor Gilinsky. 2001. *Neglected steps: The Agreed Framework's nonproliferation and nuclear safety provisions: A Nonproliferation Policy Education Center (NPEC) trip report of Discussions held in Japan and South Korea, 27 February to 2 March 2001.* Presented before an American Enterprise Institute-NPEC sponsored conference: "Korea policy challenges for the new administration, 13 March 2001. Database. Available from http://www.wizard.net/~npec/ koreatripreport.htm. Internet. Accessed on 23 August 2001.

Spector, Leonard S. 1992. *Deterring regional threats from nuclear proliferation.* Carlisle, PA: US Army War College, Strategic Studies Institute (SSI).

Sublette, Carey. 1999. *Nuclear weapons frequently asked questions.* Database. Available from http://www.milnet.com/milnet/nukeweap/Nfaq1.html. Internet. Accessed on 11 January 2002.

Snyder, Scott. 1999. *Negotiating on the edge.* Washington DC: United States Institute of Press.

Suh, Dae Sook, and Lee Chae Jin. 1998. *North Korea after Kim Il Sung.* Boulder, CO and London, England. Lynne Rienner Publisher, Inc.

Turabian, Kate L. 1996. *A manual for writers. 6th ed.* Chicago: University of Chicago Press.

United Nations Security Council. 1991. Security Council Resolution (SCR) 687. Database. Available from http://www.iaea.org/worldatom/Documents/Legal/ unsc687.shtml. Internet. Accessed on 12 January 2002.

_____. 1991. Security Council Resolution (SCR) 825. Database. Available from http://www.iaea.org/worldatom/Documents/Legal/unsc825.shtml. Internet. Accessed on 12 January 2002.

United States Congress. Senate. 1994. Senator McCain of Arizona speaking on the United States policy and crisis in Korea. S6245 (24 May). Database. Available from http://www.fas.org/spp/starwars/congress/1994/s940524-dprk.htm. Internet. Accessed on 11 January 2002.

United States Congress. Senate. 1998. *Foreign Operations, Export Financing, and Related Program Appropriations Act of 1999.* 105th Cong., 2nd sess., S 2334. Database. Available from http://thomas.loc.gov. Internet. Accessed on 11 January 2002.

United States Defense Intelligence Agency. 1991. Defense Intelligence Assessment, mobile short-range ballistic missile targeting in Operation Desert Storm. Washington DC: National Security Archives, November.

United States Department of the Army, US Army Command and General Staff College. 2001. *C/M/S 500, Fundamentals of operational warfighting: DJMO selected readings book.* Fort Leavenworth, KS: USACGSC.

United States Department of Defense. 1992. Conduct of the Persian Gulf War, The Final Report to the US Congress by the US Department of Defense. Washington, DC:

_____. 2000. Joint Pub 1-02 *Department of Defense Dictionary of Military and Associated Term.* Washington DC: US Government Printing Office.

_____. 1997. *Proliferation: Threat and response.* Washington DC: US Government Printing Office.

_____. 2001. *Proliferation: Threat and response.* Washington DC: US Government Printing Office.

United States Department of Energy. 2002. USDOE Information Administration, North Korea. Database. Available from http://www.eia.doe.gov/emeu/cabs/nkorea.html. Internet. Accessed on 11 January 2002.

United States Department of State. 2002. *Congressional budget justification: Foreign operations fiscal year 2002.* Washington DC: Office of the Secretary of State Resources, Plans and Policy

United States General Accounting Office, Resources, Community, and Economic Development Division. 1998. *Nuclear nonproliferation: Difficulties in accomplishing IAEA's activities in North Korea.* Washington DC: GAO.

_____. 1991. *National defense authorization act for fiscal year 1993, conference report to accompany H.R.2100, House of Representatives Report 102-311.* Washington DC: GAO.

United States Nuclear Regulatory Commission. 1983. *Standard Review Plan.* Nuclear Regulation (NUREG) 0800. Washington, DC: Office of Nuclear Reactor Regulation.

United States President. 1993. Letter to congressional leaders reporting on Iraq's compliance with United Nations Security Council Resolutions. (19 January). Washington DC: Database. Available from http://bushlibrary.tamu.edu/papers/1993/93011907.html. Internet. Accessed on 11 January 2002.

Vick, Charles P. 2001. WMD Around the World, North Korean Missiles. *Federation of American scientists.* Washington DC: Federation of American Scientists. Database. Available from http://www.fas.org/ nuke/guide/dprk/missile/index.html. Internet. Accessed on 11 January 2002.

Vogelaar, Marc. 2001. *The future of KEDO.* NY: Korean Peninsula Energy Development Organization. Database. Available from http://www.kedo.org/ future.htm. Internet. Accessed on 8 August 2001.

Von Hippel, David, and Peter Hayes. 1997. *DPRK Energy Sector: Current status and scenarios for 2000 and 2005.* Database. Available from http://www.nautilus.org/papers/energy/ dvh%5Fhayesscenarios.html. Internet. Accessed on 18 August 2001.

Von Hippel, David, Peter Hayes, Masami Nakata, Timothy Savage, and Chris Greacen. 2001. *Modernizing the US-DPRK Agreed Framework: The energy imperative.* Database. Available from http://www.nautilus.org. Internet. Accessed on 11 January 2002.

Walpole Robert. 2002. *CIA national intelligence estimates of foreign missile development and the ballistic missile threat through 2015.* Washington DC: Central Intelligence Agency. Database. Available from http://www.senate.gov/~gov_affairs/031102walpole.pdf. Internet. Accessed on 13 March 2002.

Watts, Barry D., and Thomas A. Keaney. 1993. *Part II: Effects and effectiveness in Gulf War air power survey.* Washington DC: US Government Printing Office.

Weissman, Steve, and Herbert Krosney. 1981. *The Islamic bomb: The nuclear threat to Israel and the Middle East.* NY: Times Books.

Wendt, James C. 1994. *The North Korean nuclear program: What is to be done?* Santa Monica, CA: RAND.

Wilborn, Thomas L. 1995. *Strategic implications of the US -DPRK Framework Agreement.* Carlisle Barracks, PA: US Army War College, Strategic Studies Institute (SSI).

Wilkening, Dean, and Kenneth Watman. 1995. *Nuclear deterrence in a regional context.* Santa Monica, CA: RAND.

Wit, Joel. 1999. The Korean Peninsula Energy Development Organization: Achievements and challenges. *The Nonproliferation Review* 6, no. 2 (winter): 59-69. Database. Available from http://cns.mis.edu/pubs/npr. Internet. Accessed on 11 August 2001.

Zhebin, Alexander. 2000. A political history of Soviet-North Korean nuclear cooperation. Pg. 27-37. Edited by James Clay Moltz and Alexandre Y. Mansourov. *The North Korea nuclear program: Security, strategy, and new perspectives from Russia.* NY: Routledge.

www.ingramcontent.com/pod-product-compliance
Lightning Source LLC
Chambersburg PA
CBHW081832280526
45789CB00007B/2436